Creations and Recreations of
The African Family in the U.S.A.
Inventions, Science and Industry

Albert Morris

Albert Morris, New York

Artists Credits:
Kay Brown, Abdul Rahman, Otto Neals, Ademola Olugebefola,
James Sepyo, Abdullah Aziz, Rod Ivey

To my ancestors, parents, family, friends and the Weusi Artists; for their spirit, purpose and drive.

Albert Morris

Editor's Note:

The material in this book is a compilation of many, many years of research and collection of articles from various sources. Whenever possible, and whenever available, I tried to give credit to the author or publisher for his or her work. In no way do I lay claim to the authorship of any of the articles that I have compiled and edited in this book. Any similarity in reference to persons, places or events mentioned in this book is purely coincidental.

Contents

FOREWORD

The achievements of African-Americans have been a vital force in Human Development throughout the centuries on the North American continent. Areas in which "The African Family" in North America has made great contributions are: Inventions, Science, and Industry. **Mr. Albert Morris** gathered and held on to Newsprints and published deeds showing in a small way, major contributions that should have been included in textbooks, alongside major-minor contributions of other U.S. citizens who were achievers in Invention, Science and Industry.

Mr. Morris made a decision to publish this book, "Creations and Recreations of The African Family in the U.S.A.", and that Family's Creation/Recreations in Inventions, Science and Industry. The title reveals an important message that The African Family has made important contributions to the everyday lives of the World's People.

Mr. Morris makes available information that will ensure that Generations of African-Americans connect the importance of their elders and foreparents with their day-to-day lives, and thereby Freedom of Power to those First World Nations called "Third World Nations".

In his book Mr. Morris projects many of the hundreds of inventions that are patented by African-American Inventors, Scientists and Industrialists. Mr. Morris has compiled, written, researched, edited and continuously updated this book since 1975. This new edition includes a very special person known to Mr. Morris; our fallen Astronaut, Ronald E. McNair, who made a notable labor of Love to all citizens of the U.S.

Those people who project, as well as, accept the premise that African-Americans' only achievements were limited to slave labor, crass labor and performing tasks so menial, as to be avoided by others. Even such menial labor must be viewed as a direct vital contribution, enabling the U.S. to have the capital to enter the Industrial Revolution in all of its stages; thus allowing the U.S. to make history in commerce, industry and technology.

A sincere "Thank You" to Mr. A. Morris.

Mr. Morris wishes to acknowledge all contributions and contributors of these works and publications.

Gaylord Hassan
Weusi Artist, Inc., NYC

"Each generation, out of relative obscurity, must discover its mission, and either fulfill it, or, betray it."

–Frantz Fanon

Isaiah Emanuel Morter, 1850's............April 7, 1924

Farmer and Philanthropist

Isaiah Emanuel Morter was born in British Honduras, (modern Belize) to very poor parents. He grew up fighting all oppositions and difficulties surrounding one born to his conditions, until he elevated himself to the highest pinnacle of service to his race and to his country. In Morter's mature years, he accumulated a fair portion of wealth, which he attributed mainly to his thriftiness and honest hard work.

Mr. Morter bequeathed $100,000 in property in Belize, Central America to the cause of African Redemption, that is the UNIA-African Communities Leagues International. Sir Isaiah Emanuel Morter, was dubbed Knight Commander of the DSO of Ethiopia by the UNIA-African Communities Leagues in the 1920's. U.S.A.

2

"He, unlike the majority of Negroes (Blacks) who accumulate wealth, did not seek to find association socially and otherwise among other races, but he was satisfied to confine his sucess to his race and give his race credit for everything that he accomplished." (Philosophy and Opinions of the Hon. Marcus Garvey, Vol. II, page 91, compiled by Amy J. Garvey, 1925) Morter contributed to, and he was a founder of The Morter Medical and Dental College, Belize City, Belize, Central America.

Why mention Isaiah E. Morter, when he wasn't born in the U.S.A.? Because, the Creations-Recreations of The African Family in most of North America, South and Central America, and the Caribbean Basin have been lost to true posterity. Jan E. Matzeliger born in 1852 in then Dutch Guiana (Modern Surinam), South America, emigrated to the U.S.. His shoe lasting machine convoluted and revolutionized the entire shoe industry in the 1900's. Inventions by The African Family in the Americas are literally in the thousands of scientific, technologic and real inventions.

The Patent Laws and Trademark Statutes[2] provide a means of protecting inventive genius in most fields. Inventors may be young, old, male, female, sole, joint, an alien, famous or otherwise, regardless of ethnic group, creed or color, vocation or interest.

Black inventors and women have ownership of patents and trademarks, which properties are issued through examination and registration procedures, respectively. This will be focused upon in this writing.

PART I

Black Innovators

Black patentees have been present since 1821 and perhaps earlier during the period when American Colonies and States issued patents before the Federal Act.[3] The number of black inventors or patentees has increased quite substantially since the first popular list by Henry E. baker in 1900 for the Paris International Exposition.[4] It listed 370 inventions of nearly 200 black inventors. From about 1950, the number has multiplied many, many times, especially during the present era of

[2] The Patent Laws (35 U.S.C. 101) state that whoever invents or discovers any new and useful process, machine, manufacture, or composition of matter or any new and useful improvement thereof, may obtain a patent therefor, subjet to the conditions and requirements of Title 35 of the United States Code. A trademark, defined in section 45 of the Trademark Act of 1946 (15 U.S.C. 1127), "includes any word, name, symbol, or device, or any combination thereof adopted and used by a manufacturer or merchant to identify his goods and distinguish them from those manufactured or sold by others." The primary functon of a trademark is to indicate origin.

The U.S. Patent and Trademark Office issues three types of patents. They are utility patents (i.e. having a use), plant patents (certain asexually reproduced plats), and design patents (designs for ornamental objects). Trademarks (marks of the trade) are issued under a registration system.

[3]The Colonial and State patents were issued only by special acts of legislature. Having no general laws to provide for the granting of patents, it was necessary for an inventor to make a special appeal to the governing body of his colony or State. The Constitution under the United States enabled Congress to enact the first patent law on April 10, 1790, from which the modern patent system has gradually evolved.

[4]The International Exposition of 1900, held in Paris, France, contained a "Negro Section" which was organized by William Edward Burghardt DuBois, educator and founder of the CRISES magazine, organ of the National Association for the Advancement of Colored People (NAACP).

Reprinted from the "Journal of the Patent Office Society" February, 1980, Vol. 62, No. 2

Mother & Child - Kay Brown

Equal Employment Opportunity.[5] Black innovators and those blacks who hold patents on their inventions[6] are a group not well recognized nor believed known in its entirety at this moment.

How is it known whether a patentee belongs to one ethnic group or another–for the laws were not drafted (nor should they be so drafted) to distinguish the same? Most of the investigative procedures are a painstaking, arduous and time-consuming task. Inquiries can be made of patent attorneys and agents; patent examiners can be questioned; known black inventors can be asked about others; and many publications can be perused for any possible hint. Thus, a list of patentees evolves from the conscientious efforts of authors who care. Some are listed as an appendix in this paper.

Historically, a legal issue arose–could a slave hold a patent? The issue of whether a non-free black had a right to hold patents apparently did not arise until 1857, when it was provoked by a letter to the Secretary of the Interior. On August 25, 1857, Oscar J. O. Stuart, a citizen of Mississippi, asked if the master of a slave could procure a patent for a useful invention discovered by his slave.[7] The question being a new one to the Secretary was submitted to the Attorney General. On June 10, 1858, Attorney General Jeremiah S. Black of Pennsylvania rendered an opinion that a new and useful machine invented by a slave could not be patented. He thus resolved it in favor of the free individual, and those not free were neglected.

It is interesting to note that on May 17, 1861, the Statutes at Large of the Confederate States of America provided for the disadvantaged slave by enacting a provision that a slave shall receive a patent for his discovery or invention and have all the rights entitled by law. This came about when Jefferson Davis also attempted to patent an invention by one of his slaves before the Civil War[8]. However, it appeared that no slave had taken

[5]In a soon to be published manuscript entitled "The Black Inventor From 1821 - 1977," by Dr. Mae P. Claytor, deceased, an in depth and the most comprehensive study was done on blacks who hold U.S. Patents and Trademarks.

[6]Sometimes referred to as the Colored inventor, or theNegro inventor in early literature.

[7] John Boyle, Patents and Civil Rights in 1857-8," 42 J. Pat. Off. Soc'y 789 (1960).

[8]Documents and massive ledgers of the Patent Office of the Confederacy are found in The Museum of the Confederacy at Richmond, Virginia. The ledgers are all written in 19th Century script covering hundreds of pages. Only 266 patents were granted between 1861 and 1864.

advantage of this act according to the records maintained by the Confederate Patent Office.[9] Perhaps some applied but were not successful.

The earliest known (pre Civil War) patent granted to a black was to Thomas L. Jennings in 1821 on March 3 as reported by C. R. Gibbs in *Afro-American Inventor* (1975). Jennings obtained a utility patent for an invention on dry scouring of clothes, which invention was proudly cited in the *Anglo-African Magazine*, volume 1, in 1859.

The next known patent to be issued to a black, after a 13 year interval, was to Henry Blair from Montgomery County, Maryland. Blair received two utility patents, one on October 14, 1834, on a seed planter and another on August 31, 1836, on a cotton platner.[10]

Although not in great abundance, black inventors continud to patent into the 1900's through the 1940's, steadily increasing by the early fifties. In some instances inventors of unusual circumstances obtained patents. John Arthur Johnson, [11] the famous black pugilist, was given a patent on an improved type of monkeywrench on April 15, 1922, while incarcerated in Leavenworth prison for violating the Mann Act.

Contrary to historical and popular belief in literature, George Washington Carver had been awarded three patents: one on a cosmetic and process of producing on January 6, 1925; a second on June 9, 1925, for paint and stain and process of producing; and a third on June 14, 1927, for a process of producing paints and stains.[12]

[9] From yearly lists at The Museum of the Confederacy Library, Richmond. Also see, Max W. Tucker, "The Patent Office of the Confederacy", 3 J. Pat. Off. Soc'y 596 (1920).

[10] U.S. Patent and Trademark Office, Digest of Patents, Index, 1790-1839, p. 469. Jennings was free and apparently so was Blair or else he would not have been awarded U.S. Patents.

[11] Otherwise known as "Jack Johnson" whose life is the subject of the film "The Great White Hope" starring James Earl Jones in the title role as "Jack Johnson.

[12] In an exhibit sponsored by Monsanto Company of St. Louis, Mo. beginning in 1978, Carver is highlighted. It is entitled "George Washington Carver: Cookstove Chemist." More information can be obtained from the Association of Science-Technology Centers in Washington, DC.

There have been and still are a few success stories concerning blacks who have sustained but overcome the frustrations of an unpredictable economy. As *Black Enterprise*, itself a ten year sucessful endeavor by its owner, Earl G. Graves, puts it in the June 1976 issue, ". . . the history of black business development in America, by and large, has been the history of individual achievement . ."[13] Perhaps this can be said of all really successful inventors or individual businessmen, but this article is not intended for the serious student of the economic history of blacks or women in the United States.

Literature has a flair for highlighting the inventions of more well-known black inventors appearing to have been successful, and whose inventions were well exploited by others. However, they died in virtual poverty or were just barely comfortable. These include Jan Matzeliger who invented the shoe lasting machine that changed the shoe industry monumentally, Granville T. Woods who worked with Thomas Alva Edison in the field of electricity, and Norbert Rillieux, inventor of the vacuum pan that revolutionized the sugar industry.

A recent illustration of a black who has utilized another form of intellectual property mentioned earlier–the trademark–is found in the diligent, hard working efforts of Henry G. Parks of Baltimore, Maryland. His firm, H.G. Parks, Inc., producer of meat products, obtained trademarks on the word "PARKS."® Parks' products–sausages are probably the best known–can be found in most supermarkets across the country. Under the leadership of Henry G. Parks, the company has been continually cited by *Black Enterprise* as one of the top 100 black firms in the country. However, to date, the company is under a new corporate structure.

One black who has struggled to make a success of his business built on the patent and trademark systems from the some 80 patents and trademarks he has received is Meredith C. Gourdine.[14]

13 "200 Years of Economic Development" by Pat Patterson, pp. 99-107.
14 Dr. Gourdine has a degree in Engineering from the California Institute of Technology. He won a Silver Medal in the broad jump at the 1952 Olympics.

Gourdine began as Gourdine Systems Inc., but he is now owner and head of the firm called Energy Innovations, Inc. of East Orange, New Jersey. He invented the "INCINERAID,"® a device that controls smoke pollution, and the Electradyne paint spray gun. Some of his inventions have been licensed to Sherwin-Williams. The Estey Corporation manufactures and sells some of his products.

Several organizations have been established to assist and help black inventors obtain patents, trademarks, and also copyrights. One is the National Patent Law Association, P. O. Box 8700, Washington, DC 20011, a non-profit organization designed to insure further growh of minority participation in proprietary rights and to educate minority business people in each area. Another is the National Business League, 4324 Georgia Avenue, Washington, DC 20011, which helps to identify markets for creations of inventors.

In Misery Born - Abdul Rahman

Benjamin Banneker

Inventor, Mathematician, Astronomer
1731 -1806

Benjamin Banneker's mechanical inventiveness led him, in 1761, to construct the first clock that was made totally in North America. It was a wooden striking clock so accurate that it kept perfect time and struck each hour unfailingly for more than 20 years. This beautiful clock was known of, by all the people in the vicinity where he lived, and people from all over travelled to see it.

He and his family owned land in Ellicott, Maryland. They farmed the land on their own and were able to provide quite well for all their needs. Benjamin Banneker's grandfather and father were both born in Africa, and they taught him an appreciation of African religion and astronomy. He attended a private school for several years and was taught by a black teacher even though it was a Quaker school.

After receiving the equivalent of an eight-grade education, he set out to educate himself in the areas of mathematics, mechanics, agriculture, astronomy, poetry, science, conversation, and surveying. Because of his great aptitude in these areas, people in the community, who were mostly white, came to him for advice and assistance with aspects of their lives and businesses related to mathematics. His father had also taught the whites how to irrigate their farms. This knowledge he brought with him from Africa.

In 1789 Benjamin Banneker's calculations had enabled him to predict a solar eclipse. Within a few years he began publishing an Almanac which contained tide tables, data and future eclipses, and a listing of useful medicinal products and formulas.

Because he was aware of the prevailing attitude of the time that Black people were ignorant and incapable of thought and higher learning, Banneker published an Almanac each year for 10 years. He used it as a means of educating the whites as to the intelligence of Black African people.

Because of his exceptional mental abilities, Banneker, a black man, was asked to join a team of six people to survey and lay out the plans for the city of Washington, D. C. After a fist fight with George Washington, the Chairman of the committee resigned and retuned to France, taking the plans with him. It was the black member of the committee, Benjamin Banneker, who was able to reproduce the exact plans.

In addition, Banneker surveyed the area of Washington, D. C. on his own. He would rise early in the morning and stay awake most of the night in order to plot the movement of the stars and other heavenly bodies, as his calculations had to be based on this data. It is apparent that if the government had been able to find a white man to do this intricate and difficult work, Banneker would not have been chosen for this prestigious job. His role is often underplayed; and, the records of his actual contributions were destroyed when someone set his house on fire the day that he was buried. His beautiful clock was also lost in the fire.

James Forten, Sr.

Inventor/Entrepreneur
1766-1842

James Forten, Sr. was born in Philadelphia, Pennsylvania, on September 2, 1766, of free black parents. His grandparents were brought to America as slaves from Africa.

Young James was educated in the colored childrens' free school of Anthony Benezet, a Quaker Abolitionist. At the age of eight, he began working alongside his father in a Philadelphia sail loft, owned by Robert Bridges, a sailmaker. Due to his father's untimely death caused by a boating accident, James was forced to take on additional work to support his family. In addition, his education came to an abrupt end at the age of ten.

At the age of 14, during the Revolutionary War, James signed up to work as a powder boy aboard the Royal Louis sailing ship. When this ship was captured by the British, he was imprisoned for seven months. Upon his release, he returned to work in the sail loft of Robert Bridges. When Bridges retired, Forten bought the company from him.

Forten began experimenting with different types of sails for ships. He finally invented a design of the canvas sail, which was better suited for guiding ships, as well as maintaining greater speed. Even though James Forten, Sr. did not patent his invention, he became one of the most successful and prosperous businessmen in the sail making industry. He accumulated considerable wealth from his invention, much of which he used to promote abolitionists causes.

Norbert Rillieux

Inventor/Engineer
1806-1894

In 1845, Norbert Rillieux invented a device that was of great value to the sugar-refining industry. His invention, a vacuum evaporating pan, not only reduced the time and cost of producing sugar, but also saved many lives. It also helped to produce a better quality of sugar.

Norbert Rillieux was born in New Orleans, Louisiana on March 17, 1806, and was educated in Paris, France. In Paris he studied at L'Ecole Centrale, and at the age of twenty four became an instructor of applied mechanics at the same school.

Upon Rillieux's return to New Orleans, he saw that methods for refining sugar were tedious, slow and hazardous. The method that was being used required slaves to ladle boiling cane juice from one kettle to another which was hard and extremely dangerous. Many slaves lost their lives performing this task.In school Rillieux learned that the boiling point of liquids is reduced as atmospheric pressure is reduced. With this in mind, he felt that the sugar refining process could be done more efficiently if the cane juice was heated in a vacuum. As a result, he invented the evaporating pan.

Norbert Rillieux was granted a patent for the "vacuum evaporating pan" in 1846. His evaporating pan was in great demand by sugar refiners and plantations in Cuba, Mexico, Louisiana and the West Indies Basin. After his evaporator process was accepted in Europe, Rillieux applied his process to the sugar in beets. Fortunes were made in sugar and rum. The labor and suffering of the African Family and the Inventive genius of the African Family in the Americas, Caribbean Basin, and Central America made this possible.

Ancestral King - Otto Neals

Joseph Jo. Anderson

Inventor
1808 - Unknown

HARVESTER COMPANY
Centennial Medal
Honoring
JOE ANDERSON
Co-Inventor of the Reaper

OBVERSE   REVERSE

In the 1830's on a farming plantation in Virginia, a born inventor, Joseph Anderson, came up with an idea to mechanize the scythe, (a large curved steel blade attached to a double grip wood handle, used to cut grass and grain). He worked on an invention of multiple moving, horsepowered, cutting blades. As a result, he created the automatic reaper, a grain harvester. He set into motion the farm machine which helped to feed a nation, and the world.

Anderson's owner, Cyrus McCormick did give him some credit for the invention of the reaper, but in 1834, McCormick was granted a patent for the horsepowered version of the automatic machine himself. He also retained all of the financial benefits generated from the reaper. He continued to revise its design until 1855, and manufactured the machine in his own factories throughout his lifetime. The name, International Harvester Co., is in the "Fortune 500". This company, International Harvester, is now known as Navistar, Inc. The Field-McCormick families have become multi-millionaires during the nineteenth and twentieth centuries.

Any talents, genius, natural gifts of chattel slaves in the U.S. then, became the material gain of the slave-owner. Countless scientific, inventive, and technologic discoveries of the African Family in the Western Hemisphere have been buried in the sands of the worse form of slavery known to civilized societies.

Benjamin Bradley

Inventor
DOB - About 1830

Benjamin Bradley, born into slavery in Annapolis, Maryland around 1830, is credited with developing a steam engine for a sloop-of-war during the 1840's.

When Bradley was about 16 years old, he used two pieces of round steel, a piece of a gun barrel, some pewter, and other materials to construct a working model of a steam engine. Shortly afterwards, he began working as a helper in the Department of Experimental Philosophy at the Naval Academy at Annapolis. While there, Bradley sold his steam engine to a midshipman. He used the money that was paid to him, plus his other savings to build an engine large enough to power a sloop-of-war at the rate of sixteen knots, or twenty five miles per hour in water. Bradley accomplished this during the 1840's.

Benjamin Bradley was unable to patent his invention because of a United States Law that prohibited slaves from patenting their works. He did, however, purchase his freedom with the proceeds from his work.

Elijah McCoy

Inventor/Engineer
1843-1929

Elijah McCoy

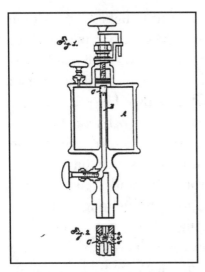

The lubrication cup which made possible the automatic oiling of machinery was invented by Elijah McCoy. His invention popularized the expression, "Real McCoy," which meant that people were getting the best equipment available.

McCoy was born in Colchester, Ontario, Canada on May 2, 1843, to run-away-slaves who fled to Kentucky before the Civil War. He was educated in Scotland as a mechanical engineer. When he returned to Canada, the only job that he could get was as a railway fireman putting wood into the furnace. He later settled in Detroit, Michigan.

After settling in Detroit, McCoy began to devise a cup that could regulate the flow of oil within moving parts of industrial machines, without necessarily stopping or shutting them down completely. His first invention was a lubricator for steam engines, for which he receive a patent on July 12, 1872. He established his own firm and obtained patents fo a total of fifty seven invention, including the lawn mower.

Lewis Howard Latimer

Inventor/Engineer
1848 -

Lewis H. Latimer

Lewis H. Latimer, a member of Thomas Edison's research team, and an assistant to Alexander Graham Bell, played a vital role in the early electronics and telephone industries.

Latimer was born in Chelsea, Massachusetts on September 4, 1848. his formal education only consisted of a few years of grammar school because of the family's financial situation at the time. Young Lewis did odd jobs to help his struggling family.

At the age of fifteen, Latimer went to fight for the Union in the Civil War. When the war was over, he became an office boy at a law firm that dealt with patents. It was here that he discovered a passion for drawing. He was a self-taught draftsman and soon began to put these skills to use. He prepared the mechanical drawings for Alexander Graham Bell's patent application for his telephone design. He later joined the Edison Electric Company where he conducted research on electrical lighting. In 1890, Latimer wrote, "Incandescent Electric Lighting," a book which became a guide for lighting engineers.

Latimer created an electic light bulb with carbon filament. This was an improvement on the bulb invented by Edison which contained a filament made of paper. He sold the patent for the Incandescent Light Bulb with Carbon Filament to the United States Electric Company in 1881. Latimer went on to patent a process for manufacturing carbon filament in 1882, and also developed a threaded wooden socket for light bulbs. He supervised the installation of public lighting in New York City, Philadelphia, Montreal and London.

Latimer's other patented inventions were: the first water closet (toilet) for railroads in 1874, and a fore-runner for the air conditioner in 1886. Although today's light bulbs no longer use filaments of carbon, Lewis Latimer will be remembered for making possible the widespread use of the electric light.

Andrew Jackson Beard

Inventor
1849-1921

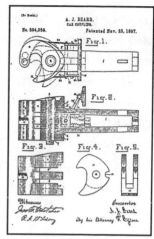

Beard's Car Couple,
Pat. #594,059 11/23/1897

Andrew Beard was born a slave in Jefferson County, Alabama in 1849. He was emancipated at the age of fifteen.

Beard was a laborer in the railroad yards at Eastlake, Alabama. While working in the railyards, he developed a device for hooking railroad cars together, or car coupling. The method being used at that time required a worker to brace himself between two cars, and drop a metal pin into place at the exact moment the cars came together. This was extremely dangerous. Many workers lost limbs, and sometimes their lives. Beard, himself, lost a leg in a car coupling accident.

Andrew Beard invented an automatic coupling device that fastened railroad cars to each other by merely bumping them together. His device was called the "Jenny Coupler". Beard was granted a patent for his Car Coupler on November 23, 1897. His invention, which was improved on in 1899, is a forerunner of the automatic coupler today.

Among Beard's other inventions are: a rotary steam engine, patented on July 5, 1892, and a plow, patented in 1881.

Jan E. Matzeliger
Inventor
1852-1889

Jan Matzeliger

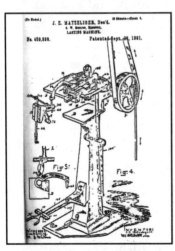

Jan Matzeliger emigrated from Surinam, (Old Dutch Guiana) South America to Lynn, Massachusetts and was employed at the Lynn Shoe Factory. Matzeliger worked endless nights in his rented room to develop and invent a lasting shoe machine, by using cigar boxes.

In March of 1883, Matzeliger was granted a patent for this machine. May of 1885, his machine turned out seventy five pairs of shoes. Previously, it took about an hour to fabricate a pair of shoes. With Matzeliger's machine this was accomplished in fifty seconds.

Thousands of new jobs were created. More people were able to afford shoes. Many white immigrants left European poverty to work and prosper in the shoe industry created by Jan Matzeliger, a black inventor. The majority of Matzeliger's race was existing in hell, and abject poverty during the end of the last century. Matzeliger's invention saw U.S. shoe exports "boom" into the millions of pairs, imported the world over.

Granville T. Woods

Inventor
1856-1910

One of the most prolific inventors of the African Family in Kidnapped Captivity, U.S.A. was Granville T. Woods. Woods had over thirty five patents for electro-mechanical systems and devices that developed new energy techniques for communication, transportation and the earliest computers. Woods was responsible for over 100 inventions vital to a Modern Society.

Granville T. Woods was born in Columbus, Ohio on April 23, 1856. He had little formal education, and as a result of his parents being poor working people, Woods became an apprentice in a railroad yard blacksmith shop. The Woods family migrated to the state of Missouri where Granville worked in a variety of jobs which gave him the background, teaching, and experience to begin to develop his inventions.

In 1884, he secured a patent number for a furnace and boiler to produce steam heat. Woods invented and improved the telephone transmitter. The electric trolley car powered by overhead wires was made practical, plus the grooved wheel for the trolley car. The "third rail" revolutionized mass commuter travel in medium and large metro areas. An improved air-brake system, more commonly known as the Automatic Airbrakes, was invented June 10, 1902.

Woods invented a telegraph system that enabled moving trains on heavy and light railroad systems to communicate with each other. This invention enhanced a better rail safety. Woods sold most of his inventions to General Electric Corp., Westinghouse, Con-Edison and Bell Telephone Companies.

Granville T. Woods invented the incubator. He electrified the earlier desk calculators leading to early generation computers. He was involved

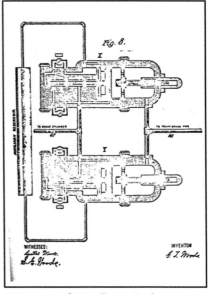

Diagram of Wood's Air Brake system

for some years with a Dr. Crocker, for prior rights for an electric corporation in Cleveland, Ohio. Therefore, Woods set-up one of the early corporations of The African Family in our sojourn in the U.S.A.

Woods invented the basic Electric Railway System, by which all subway trains are being run. Woods was responsible for the "Metal Shoe", and the Third Rail, which was also his creation. His invention did away with horse-drawn and steam-operated railway in the budding commuter and mass transit systems of the metropolitan cities of the U.S. The general acceptance of Mr. Woods' electric railway triggered Edison's street-lighting plan being put into use.

List of Patents Issued to Granville T. Woods

Electro-Mechanical Brake	Aug. 16, 1887	368,265
Overhead Conduct System for Electric Railroad	May 29, 1888	383,844
Electromotive R.R System	June 26, 1888	385,034
Tunnel Constr. For Subway	July 17, 1888	386,282
Galvanic Battery	Aug.14, 1888	387,839
Automatic Safety Cut-out for Electric Circuits	Jan. 1, 1889	395,535
Electric Rail System	Nov. 10, 1891	463,020
Electric Rail Supply System	Oct. 31, 1893	507,606
Electric Rail Conduit	Nov. 21, 1893	509,065
System of Electric Distribution	Oct.31, 1896	639,692
Railway Telegraph	Nov. 15, 1887	373,383
Induction Telegraph	Nov. 29, 1887	373,915

Halle Tanner Dillon Johnson

Physician
1864-1901

Halle Tanner Dillon Johnson was born in Pittsburgh, Pennsylvania in 1864. She grew up in Philadelphia, where her home was a popular gathering place for Black intellectuals.

After high school, she worked with her father, Bishop Benjamin Tucker Tanner, on a newspaper published by the African Methodist Episcopal (A.M.E.) Church.

She married Charles Dillon of New Jersey. Her joy, however, was cut short by his unexpected death and the young widow returned to Philadelphia with her daughter, Sadie.

At age twenty four, she decided to become a doctor and enrolled in Women's Medical School. She was the only Black person in her class of thirty six and graduated with honors.

After finishing medical school, she faced the dilemma of where to practice medicine. She decided to join Booker T. Washington at Tuskegee Institute in Alabama.

At the urging of Washington, she agreed to sit for the Alabama Medical Board Examination. She studied with Dr. Cornelius Dorsett, Alabama's first licensed Black doctor.

The examination was difficult and took ten days. However, Johnson triumphed, becoming one of the first women to pass the Medical Board in the state of Alabama.

At Tuskegee Institute, she established a nursing school. She also staffed the Lafayette Dispensary, which provided medical care for students and for community residents.

She later married the Reverend John Quincy Johnson, a mathematics teacher. They relocated to South Carolina when he was named president of Allen University.

Prof. Matilda Evans

Surgeon
1869-1935

One of the female physicians that was honored in the retrospective: Women Doctors in America – 1835-1920; at the New York Academy of Medicine; 2 East 103rd Street, in New York City, was Dr. Matilda Evans.

The exhibit explored the dramatic history of women's entry into American medicine; their great success in the 19th century; their numerical decline after 1900; and their relatively recent professional success.

Dr. Evans was the first African American woman to be licensed as a physician in the state of South Carolina. She opened the first hospital for African Americans in Columbia, South Carolina, and introduced the idea of providing free medical examinations for public school children. She also opened a training school for nurses. In 1918 Dr. Evans became a registered volunteer on the Medical Service Corps of the United States Army.

George Washington Carver

Scientist
1864-1943

Probably the best known black scientist and inventor is George Washington Carver, who alone, nearly revolutionized agriculture in the South. At a time when the South's major crop, cotton, was faced with total destruction by the boll weevil; Dr. Carver, through scientific experiments showed the South that peanuts, soy-beans and sweet potatoes (yams), among other crops, should be planted, along with cotton. If one crop failed, there would be others from which farmers could make money. Known as the Wizard of Tuskegee," Dr. Carver developed hundreds of products from the peanut, the soybean, the pecan, the sweet potato, and even from weeds. Today, there are many schools and other institutions named in memory of Dr. Carver.

George Washington Carver devoted his life to research projects connected primarily with southern agriculture. The products he derived from the peanut and the soybean revolutionized the economy of the South by liberating it from an excessive dependence on cotton.

Born a slave in Diamond Grove, Missouri, Carver was only an infant when he and his mother were abducted from his owner's plantation by a band of slave raiders. His mother was sold andshipped away, but her son was ransomed by his master in exchange for a race horse.

26

At the age of thirteen, Carver was already on his own. By working as a farm hand, he managed to obtain a high school education. He was admitted as the first black student of Simpson College, Indianola, Iowa. He then attended Iowa Agricultural College (now Iowa State University) where, while working as the school janitor, he receved a degree in agricultural science in 1894. Two years later he received a master's degree from the same school and became the first black to serve on its faculty. Within a short time his fame spread, and Booker T. Washington offered him a post at Tuskegee.

Dr. Carver never patented any of the many discoveries he made. While at Tuskegee, saying "God gave them to me, how can I sell them to someone else?" In fact, in 1938 he donated over $30,000 of his life's savings to the George Washington Carver Foundation. The rest of his estate was willed to the organization, so his work might he carried on after his death.

Carver is buried alongside Booker T. Washington. His epitaph reads: "He could have added fortune to fame, but caring for neither, he found happiness and honor in being helpful to the world."

Synthetic Products Developed By Carver

Adhesives	Metal Polish
Axle Grease	Milk Flakes
Bleach	Mucilage
Buttermilk	Paper
Cheese	Rubbing Oils
Chili Sauce	Salve
Cream	Soil Conditioner
Creosote	Shampoo
Dyes	Shoe Polish
Flour	Shaving Cream
Fuel Briquettes	Sugar
Ink	Synthetic Marble
Instant Coffee	Synthetic Rubber
Insulating Board	Talcum Powder
Linoleum	Vanishing Cream
Mayonnaise	Wood Stains
Meal	Wood Filler
Meat Tenderizer	Worchestershire Sauce

John Standard

Inventor
D.O.B - unknown

The modern home refrigerator of the 1890's was the "Brain-Child" of John Standard. On July 14, 1891, Standard, an African American inventor of Newark, New Jersey, was granted a patent # 455, 891, for his improved design of the refrigerator. On October 29, 1889, John Standard was also granted a Patent # 413,689 for an oil stove invention.

Fred Patterson

Automobile Designer/ Manufacturer
1869-1937

Frederick Douglas Patterson was the first African-American car designer and manufacturer. In 1915 he manufactured his first car, the Patterson-Greenfield (name given their line of cars) Motorcar which came in two models: a roadster, and a big four door touring car.

During the early 1900's there were scores of automobile manufacturers competing for a piece of the vehicle market. An African American company, C.R. Patterson & Son Carriage Company of Greenfield , Ohio made its mark in this industry. This company was the world's first and only African American founded and owned automobile manufacturing company. The owner C.R. Patterson & Son was, Frederick Patterson's father, Charles Richard Patterson. Reports have it that Charles Patterson was born into slavery on a plantation in Virginia but escaped to freedom in Ohio in 1861.

After the death of his father, Frederick took over the operation of the company. He began to see that there were more and more of the "horseless carriages," or automobiles, on the road. After noticing how the demand for cars had increased over a seven year period, he felt that it was time to build a Patterson car. On September 23, 1915, the first Patterson-Greenfield car was manufactured. This car was priced at $850. During this time (1900-1926), the Patterson-Greenfield car was in direct competition with the Hudson, Essex, Packard, Nash and Hupmobile.

C.R. Patterson & Son began as manufacturer of carriages but in the end, they were manufacturing automobiles, buses and trucks. Their buses in large numbers were the first to travel the streets of Cincinnati, Ohio. Many of the Patterson -Greenfield cars were shipped as far away as Haiti and Mexico.

Garrett A. Morgan

Inventor
1877-1963

Garrett A. Morgan, born in Paris, Kentucky in 1877, received wide recognition for his outstanding contributions to public safety. In the early 1900's firemen in many cities wore the safety helmet and gas mask that he invented. Morgan's gas inhaler became the life-saving gas mask worn by troops during WWI and WWII.

On July 25, 1916, Morgan used his invented mask (gas) to dive 200 feet below Lake Erie to rescue thirty two men trapped by an underwater explosion in a tunnel being constructed under Lake Erie. The city of Cleveland honored Morgan with a gold medal award for his heroic efforts. The 2nd International Exposition of Safety in N.Y., 1914, presented Morgan an award for the invention of his helmet and gas mask.

Morgan invented world moving items in two separate categories: 1912, the gas inhaler (medium for the gas mask); and in 1923, his more famous automated three-way, electric stoplight which changed the control of motor traffic throughout the world. The red-stop, the amber-caution and the green-go signal lights were also Morgan's creations. Some years later, Morgan sold his design rights to General Electric Corp.

Dr. Ernest Everett Just

Scientist
1883-1941

Cell biologist, Dr. Just, is regarded as one of this country's most distinguished biological scientists. He was a meticulous worker in biological research who complemented theory with extensive experimentation. His major interests were fertilization and development of the eggs of marine animals.

After graduation as valedictorian of his prep school class at Kimball Union Academy in Meriden, N.H., he went on to receive degrees in both history and biology from Dartmouth. He was elected to Phi Beta Kappa in his junior year and was the only student in his class to graduate magna cum laude. He also received a Ph.D. degree in zoology, magna cum laude, from the University of Chicago.

In addition to teaching at Howard Univevsity, Dr. Just devoted a considerable part of his career to doing research in such prestigious institutions as the Marine Biological Laboratory in Woods Hole, Mass.; the Kaiser Wilhelm Institute in Berlin, Germany; the Stazione Zoologica in Naples, Italy; and at France's Station Biologique at Roscoff. A prolific writer who shared the results of his painstaking research with fellow scientists, Dr. Just produced approximately 70 separate research papers on fertilization and experimental embryology, some of which were done in cooperation with his graduate students. His major works include *The Biology of the Cell Surface and Basic Methods for Experiments in Eggs of Marine Animals,* both published in 1939. In 1915 he was the first recipient of the Spingarn Medal of the NAACP.

Reprinted from: CIBA-GEIGY Corp. pamphlet "Exceptional Black Scientists"

Archie Alexander

Engineer
1888-1958

Archie Alexander, a design and construction engineer, left his creations on the landscape of the U.S. by building bridges, freeways, airfields, railroad trestles and power-plants.

Born in Ottumwa, Iowa, Alexander, attended the State University and earned a degree in engineering in 1912. He and a former classmate established their own engineering firm and constructed major projects across the nation, after Alexander spent several years as a design engineer. At home, they built the heating plant and powerhouse at the University of Iowa, a sewage treatment plant in Grand Rapids, Michigan, an airfield in Tuskegee, Alabama, and the Tidal Basin Bridge and seawall and the Whitehurst Freeway in Washington, D.C.

In 1954 President Dwight Eisenhower of the U.S., appointed Alexander Territorial Governor of the American Virgin Islands.

David Crosthwait

Inventor
1891-1976

Crosthwait received a B.S. degree in mechanical engineering in 1913. He received thirty four U.S. patents and eighty foreign patents relating to the design, installation, testing and servicing of powerplants, heating and ventilating systems.

Crosthwait worked for the Dunham Company of Chicago, Illinois, during much of his career and headed its research laboratory in Marshalltown, Iowa. Later, he served as technical advisor to the company.

He was an authority on heat transfer, ventilation and air-conditioning. Crosthwait invented several new systems. He developed the control systems and the variable vacuum system of heating and ventilating for major buildings-including Rockefeller Center, in New York City. His writings included a manual on heating and cooling with water and guides, standards and codes dealing with heating, ventilation, refrigeration and air-conditioning.

Crosthwait was awarded an honoraty doctoral degree in 1975 from Purdue University, the same school from which he graduated in 1913. Crosthwait continued to teach a course in steam heating theory and controls at Purdue University after retiring from the industry.

Frederick M. Jones

Inventor
1893-1961

One sees hundreds of refrigerated trucks rolling across this country. Frederick M. Jones developed and patented the machinery which made it all possible. His invention changed the course of the frozen food industry. The self-starting motor that Jones designed and invented, cooled, heated, froze, and defrosted food products.

Jones had workable inventions in other fields. He invented a two-cycle gas and gasoline engine, a portable x-ray machine, and a sound system for movie theaters.

Dr. Percy I. Julian

Chemist
1899-1975

Chemist Dr. Julian, the grandson of former slaves, graduated Phi Beta Kappa and valedictorian of his class from DePauw University. He became interested in soy-beans as a source of synthetic drugs while studying for his Ph.D. in Vienna. In 1935, he became the first person to synthesize the drug physostigmine from soybeans. Physostigmine is used in the treatment of glaucoma.

Dr. Julian taught chemistry at various colleges including Howard University and DePauw. He left the academic world in 1936 when he was named research director of the Glidden Company of Chicago. After 18 years with Glidden, Dr. Julian formed his own firm, Julian Laboratories, in 1954.

Among his many accomplishments was the development of a foam used to extinguish gasoline and oil fires which saved numerous lives in World War II; the discovery of a more economical way to extract sterols from soybean oil to produce sex hormones; and the development of a way of producing cortisone synthetically in large quantities at a reasonable cost. Until Dr. Julian's discovery, cortisone, which is used in the treatment of rheumatoid arthritis, was available in limited quantities and was extremely expensive.

During his career, Dr. Julian authored or co-authored numerous scientific articles and held over 100 patents. He received many awards and honors including the Spingarn Medal from the NAACP, the Chemical Pioneer Award, and 19 honorary degrees.

Reprinted from: CIBA-GEIGY Corp. pamphlet "Exceptional Black Scientists"

Solomon Harper

Inventor
1895-1980

Solomon Harper, Inventor and Electrical Engineer, was born October 8, 1895, of African and Native American ancestry on a farm near Poplar Grove, Arkansas, U.S.A.

When a youth of teen age, Harper became an inventor of devices. Of great value, were his inventions to the United States Government; on application he received patents at this age. He was forced to leave his southern home when this news circulated through the community. The scar burned on his cheek when he was a baby in his mother's arms had conditioned him to start a search for justice between people.

Harper as a youth was always tinkering with different devices. He left his home state to come to New York City, to seek greater achievements. He received a degree in engineering from Pratt Institute in Brooklyn, N.Y. about 1916.

Harper researched and developed a Blocking System for Controlling Railway Trains. He also developed the lead insulation shield for protection against X-Rays, or X-Ray Radiation. It protected the X-Ray Technician first, then, a portable shield was developed to protect the patient.

Harper researched and developed the Extreme Heat Stabilized Switch, which was used, and still utilized as part of the core of Atomic and Modern Nuclear devices. Solomon Harper was the common man's scientist-intellectual.

On May 13, 1915, he enlisted in the United States Army

and served in France during World War I, as Technical Sergeant. Between 1924 thru 1968 Mr. Harper was a newspaper correspondent. He was married and widowed.

Mr. Harper was research editor of U.S. Soil Conservation Services at Columbia University from1939-1942. He was Senior Engineering Investigator and Chief Editorial Examiner of various mechanical and electrical machines, and, also examiner of qualifications for employment in the New York State Employment Service.

Concerned always about community development and improvement, Mr. Harper was active in pressing for better housing and hospitals, counseling the unemployed, and for maintaining peace and stability. He was active as a Member of the Centennial Public Relations Committee of the Colonel Young Memorial Foundation.

In 1956 Mr. Harper proposed to the President of the United States that 5000 Native American and African Scholarships be granted in honor of Dr. George Washington Carver. Mr. Harper made many patent applications for his valuable inventions. He spent much of his life in courts until 1969, trying to get the U. S. grants of Patent Rights, which if granted, according to some researchers estimate, would aggregate in the billions of dollars.

Mr. Harper was manufacturer of metal products and design of physical and shock resistant thermostat relays. He is cited in "Who's Who in Eastern U.S.A. and in Canada 1969-1973." He is also listed in "Leaders in American Science" Vol. 4,5,6,8, in Library of Congress.

The following is a quotation from Rev. A. Merral Willis. "Mr. Harper's bitter early life and his contribution to this country and to the world in the form of numerous patents is comparable to the early life and contribution of George Washington Carver."

Mr. Harper was a member of the American Association for the Advancement of Science, and also a member of the American Preparedness Association, He was working on a book about his life at the time of his death. (from the collected notes of friends and neighbors) Harlem , New York, N.Y.

Black Man - Ademola Olugebefola

Dr. W. Montague Cobb

Anatomist and Medical Editor
1904 -1990

Anatomist and medical editor Dr. Cobb is a true Renaissance man, having enjoyed a long and distinguished career in a number of different fields. During the 51 years that he was a member of Howard University Medical School faculty, more than 5,700 medical and dental students studied in his classroom. Dr. Cobb also served as editor of the *Journal of the National Medical Association* for 28 years, developing it into a highly-respected medical publication. He has written more than 700 published works in fields as diverse as anatomy, physical anthropology, public health, medical history and medical education.

He was the first black man elected to the presidency of the American Association of Physical Anthropologists, and also served as chairman of the anthropology section of the American Association for the Advancement of Science.

Numerous awards and honors have been bestowed upon him, including the highest award of the American Association of Anatomists, and the highest civilian honor of the U.S. Navy for his ongoing effort in the fields of equal opportunity and community relations. As a member of the board of directors of the NAACP for 31 years, and its president from 1976-1982, Dr. Cobb has been influential in drawing national attention to inequities in health care.

In addition to his formal degrees (B.A., Amherst; M.D., Howard; Ph.D., Western Reserve), he has received honorary degrees from schools around the world.

Reprinted from: CIBA-GEIGY Corp. pamphlet "Exceptional Black Scientists"

Dr. Charles R. Drew

Physician
1904-1950

Physician Dr. Drew was a star athlete in high school and college who set equally impressive records in the medical field. After graduating from Amherst College, Dr. Drew was a coach, and a biology and chemistry instructor at Morgan State College. He later received his doctor of medicine and master of surgery degrees from McGill University's Medical School. He is best known for his research on blood plasma. His blood preservation discoveries led to the formation of blood banks in England and the United States during World War II. Because of his expertise in this area, he was made medical supervisor of the Plasma for Britain Project and later became director of the first American Red Cross Blood Bank.

He left the Red Cross in 1941 and became professor of surgery and director of Freedman's Hospital at Howard University Medical School. As a teacher and model for his students, Dr. Drew was without equal. During the nine years he taught at Howard, more than half of America's black surgeons who received certification from the American Board of Surgery studied directly under him.

While at Howard, Dr. Drew received honorary degrees from Virginia State College and Amherst. He also received the Spingarn Medal from the NAACP in 1944. He was one of the first black doctors selected for membership on the American Board of Surgery.

Reprinted from: CIBA-GEIGY Corp. pamphlet "Exceptional Black Scientists"

Dr. Warren E. Henry

Physicist, Education
1909-2001

Dr. Warren E. Henry's work in the area of radar technology, and his research on the physical properties of materials, earned him the praise as one of the most respected scientist in this country's history.

Dr. Henry was born on a peanut farm in Evergreen, Alabama, in 1909. His parents were both graduates of Tuskegee Institute (now Tuskegee University). As a child, he had the good fortune of meeting Dr. George Washington Carver who lived on his parent's farm doing research during the summer.

Like his parents, Warren Henry also studied at Tuskegee Institute where he majored in three subjects, mathematics, English and French. He earned a Bachelor of Science degree from Tuskegee in 1931, after which he served as a principal at a school in Ardmore, Alabama. While serving as principal he received a summer scholarship to attend Atlanta University. At the end of the summer he received a tuition scholarship to attend the same school. While at Atlanta University, he taught classes at Spelman and Morehouse Colleges, and in 1937 he earned a Master of Science degree in Organic Chemistry. He enrolled in the Ph.D program at the University of Chicago and in 1941received his doctorate degree in Physics and Physical Chemistry.

During his career, Dr. Henry associated with more than seventeen Nobel Laureates. He studied with a number of Nobel

41

Prize winners like: Dr. Arthur Compton who taught him quantum mechanics; Dr. Wolfgang Pauli taught him nuclear forces; and Robert Millikan taught him molecular spectra.

After receiving his doctorate, Dr. Henry wanted to continue his research but was unable to do so because only the historically black schools offered him a job. As a result, he returned to Tuskegee to teach. Some of his students were members of the 99th Pursuit Squadron, part of which became the Tuskegee Airmen.

In 1943 Dr. Henry was recruited by the Massachusetts Institute of Technology to work on a Navy project. There he developed amplifiers that were used on portable radar systems to detect targets like enemy submarines.

Around 1947 Dr. Henry wanted to do low temperature research but his request to use Rutgers University's equipment was turned down. In 1948 he was hired by the Naval Research Laboratory in Washington, DC, as a physicist. He remained there for twelve years. His research and knowledge of materials at extremely low temperatures was probably the best during that time.

While at Lockheed Space & Missile Company he developed guidance systems for detection of submarines, and he helped to design the Hover Craft that was developed for night fighting during the Vietnam Conflict.

Dr. Warren Henry contributed to hundreds of scientific articles, and co-authored the 1934 book "Procedures in Elementary Qualitative Chemical Analysis". In courses on solid state physics or material science, students are often introduced to Dr. Henry's work. He was a Fellow of the American Physical Society, and the American Association for the Advancement of Science. Dr Henry was also the recipient of numerous awards.

W. Lincoln Hawkins

Inventor, Chemist
1911-1992

Not so long ago, underground cables had to be replaced about every five years. This was necessary because the minerals in the earth would corrode the cables. Dr. Hawkins, along with his colleagues at Bell Laboratories, invented an anti-oxidant addictive that made possible inexpensive plastic insulation of telephone cables. This system protected the cables from weathering condition.

Dr. Hawkins was granted a total of one hundred forty seven (147) Patents relating to the development of environmentally advanced materials for communications equipment. Eighteen (18) were U.S. patents, and one hundred twenty nine (129) were foreign.

Dr. William C. Curtis

Engineer
1914-1976

William Curtis was at RCA for 23 years. Curtis had been responsible for the direction of theoretical and experimental analyses of new radar techniques. Curtis' advanced work included the famous Black-Cat Weapons System, the MG-3 Fire Control Radar, the 300-A-Weapon System Radar, Airbourne Interceptor Data Line and High Resolution Radar.

Dr. Curtis was the Dean of Engineering at Tuskegee Institute in Alabama. At Tuskegee he conducted special programs to train black pilots and black airplane mechanics during World War II.

Robert Bundy

Inventor
1912-

The top officer of the U.S. Army Signal Corp commended Robert Bundy for his work on the basic design of a man transportable radar, during WWII. These man-transportable radars were used by U.S. troops at the Normandy invasion-WWII. Bundy had investigated the principle of the travelling wave tube early in 1939. He also developed an x-ray system for detecting weapons and small wires leading to explosives being loaded onto aircraft.

Louis Roberts

Inventor
1913-1995

As director of engineering at the U.S. Transportation Center in Cambridge, Massachusetts, Louis Roberts provided a Center for transportation technology and system development; in the areas of technical planning, technical support, and program management. Louis Roberts served as professor of Physics at Howard University. Roberts holds eleven patents on electronic devices.

The Hunt Printing Company

1916 -

L. D. Stevens

The Hunt Printing Company was established in 1916 by Laurence T. Hunt. The location was 34 West 136th Street, in the basement of the building where the Hunt family lived.

Pastors and members of their congregations, physicians, attorneys, social workers, promoters, fraternal organization members and business people – all found their way to that basement because there they could obtain "clean", accurate printing at fair prices.

In 1946 Mr. Hunt's godson, Leonard Stevens, president at that time, purchased one-half interest in the business and set about modernizing the plant; installing automatic printing presses and a typesetting machine. Since then the company has had three locations, 2289 Seventh Avenue, 143 West 135th Street, and 302 West 134th Street, its present location. Rene Atkinson joined the firm in 1982 and is now its president. Through the years, management has routinely made changes in technology in a continuing effort to provide its customers with up to date, "clean" and accurate printing at fair prices. Letterpress was converted to offset production; typesetting is now done by computer; and our large two-color offset press has been replaced by an even larger four-color machine. There is also a complete bindery, including a paper cutter, folding machine and automated stitching. There is a complete pre-press department with camera, light tables, film processor and an automatic plate maker.

All this equipment is necessary to perform the quality service that is provided. More important, however, is the caliber of the staff employed. They are experienced, dedicated people determined to provide clients with the best printing services available.

Katherine C.G. Johnson

Physicist, Space Scientist,
Mathematician
1918-

Katherine Johnson received her education as a mathematician and physicist at two historically black colleges in West Virginia (Bluefield State and in Black-Bluefield State and West Virginia State). She was a key person at the National Aeronautics and Space Admin. (NASA) in the Flight Dynamics and Control Division. Ms. Johnson devised a method for tracking and mapping a space vehicle on a mission. It was her task during the peak of the space program, including the moon landings, to know where the astronauts were every second of any Lunar Spacecraft Operation. Johnson worked on absorbing problems of interplanetary trajectories, space navigation, and the orbits of spacecraft.

Dr. Lloyd N. Ferguson

Chemist
1918 -

Dr. Ferguson has engaged in a lifelong love affair with chemistry. A teacher for more than 35 years, his imaginative presentation of his subject has inspired countless students. He graduated from the University of California at Berkeley with a B.S. in chemistry and was the first black to earn a Ph.D. in chemistry from that institution. Since 1964, he has been professor of organic chemistry at California State University in Los Angeles.

His professional reputation has spread world-wide. During his 20 years on the faculty at Howard University, Dr. Ferguson's guidance led to the establishment of the first Ph.D. program in that university's history. He has written six chemistry textbooks and has had numerous articles published in professional journals and encyclopedias. His textbook *Modern Structural Theory of Organic Chemistry* is widely credited with influencing the thinking of a generation of chemists. He has earned the respect of students and colleagues alike for his work in the Minority Student Training for Biomedical Research Program at California State, Los Angeles. Dr. Ferguson's research endeavors have been in the areas of cancer chemotherapy, the relationship between structure and biological activity, and the functioning of our sense of taste. In 1981 he received the Outstanding Professor Award, a California State University System-wide honor, and has been the recipient of many national awards in chemical education.

Reprinted from: CIBA-GEIGY Corp. pamphlet "Exceptional Black Scientists"

Dr. Jane C. Wright

Cancer Researcher
1919-

Dr. Wright, daughter of Dr. Louis Wright, followed in her father's distinguished footsteps—first into medicine, later into cancer research. Motivated by the challenge to find a cure and by her concern to help cancer patients live more comfortable and worthwhile lives, she has been engaged in chemotherapy research since 1949. Dr. Wright has received numerous awards and honors for her contributions to cancer chemotherapy research, including a salute from the American Association for Cancer Research.

Dr. Wright received her A.B. from Smith College and her M.D. with honors from New York Medical College. She also has received honorary degrees from institutions such as the Women's Medical College of Pennsylvania and Denison University. After serving her internships at Bellevue Hospital and Harlem Hospital in New York City, she served on their medical and surgical staffs for many years.

Dr. Wright became assistant professor of research surgery at New York University Medical College in 1956 and adjunct associate professor there in 1961. She has been professor of surgery at New York Medical College since 1967 and is still striving to find a cure for cancer. She also served as associate dean of New York Medical College from 1967-1975, the highest post in medical administration attained at that time by a woman.

Dr. Wright has served as president of the New York Cancer Society, as a trustee of Smith College, as a fellow of the New York Academy of Medicine, and as a member of the President's Commission on Heart Disease, Cancer and Stroke.

Reprinted from: CIBA-GEIGY Corp. pamphlet "Exceptional Black Scientists"

Dr. David Blackwell

Mathematician
1919-

Dr. Blackwell is a mathematician and teacher who has been a pioneer in the field of statistics. He has served as professor of statistics at the University of California at Berkeley since 1954, establishing a distinguished record as a teacher and researcher. Dr. Blackwell specializes in the fields of set theory and the theory of games such as bridge and chess. He views mathematics as a way of thinking which disciplines the mind and changes the way people approach and analyze problems.

Born in Centralia, Ill., he received his bachelor's, master's and doctorate degrees from the University of Illinois in mathematics, an unusual field for a black person to enter in the 1930s. He then spent one year as a Rosenwald Fellow at Princeton University's prestigious Institute for Advanced Study. He began his teaching career at Southern University in Baton Rouge, La., and subsequently taught at Clark College in Atlanta, Ga., and Howard University before moving to Berkeley.

Dr. Blackwell is currently the only black member of the National Academy of Sciences. He also has served as president of both the Institute of Mathematical Statistics and the Bernoulli Society, and as vice president of the American Statistical Association. In addition, four universities have awarded him honorary doctorate degrees. A modest man with a lively sense of humor, Dr. Blackwell has published more than 80 articles about mathematics and statistics. But teaching is his first love because he enjoys seeing students—from college freshmen to graduate students—tackle and grasp new mathematical concepts.

Reprinted from: CIBA-GEIGY Corp. pamphlet "Exceptional Black Scientists"

Otis Boykin

Inventor
1920-1982

Boykin was famous for his invention of the control unit in the life-saving pacemaker, which is being worn by heart patients throughout the world. His device controls the current going to the heart, thereby, regulating the medically prescribed rate of the heartbeat. His non-inductive, wire-type flat resistor claimed two major achievements: The U.S. Government changed its own specifications in favor of this low, time-constant resistor. Next, the same flat resistor enabled manufacturers of computers to convert from analog to digital systems more efficiently. Boykin's resistors have found worldwide use in missiles, radios, televisions and spacecraft.

O.S. (Ozzie) Williams

Aeronautical Engineer
1921-

    O.S. Williams was the first black engineer to be hired by Republic Aviation, Inc.. Just before WWII, there was a major breakthrough for qualified black engineers to practice their professional specialties in the field of engineering.

    Williams later at Greer Hydraulics developed the first airbourne radar beacon for locating crashed aircraft. He joined Grumman International in 1961, where he was in charge of development and production of the control rocket systems that guided the lunar modules during moon landings. Williams was among the earliest of the African Family in North America to contribute to the U.S. space and moon programs.

John Mullin

Inventor
1921-

John Mullin, in 1974, brought his backyard paver into the construction industry. This was Mullin's "4 by 4 self-propelled utility asphalt paver" which could pave seventy five square feet per minute. This paver included a path width from six feet to a generous twelve feet. It had floating regulators which could lay a mat of asphalt from a quarter inch to six inches in thickness. Mullin was among the first of the African Family in Kidnapped Captivity in the U.S.A to design, build, and market heavy-duty equipment.

J. Ernest Wilkins Jr.

Physicist, Engineer, Mathematician
1923-

J. Ernest Wilkins

Mathematician, physicist and engineer, J. Ernest Wilkins Jr. has contributed his talents mainly to the research and development of nuclear power. As a teenager, Wilkins attracted nationwide attention when he received his college degree at seventeen years of age. Wilkins was granted his Ph.D. from the University of Chicago at nineteen. Wilkins taught mathematics and did research at the university's Metallurgical Lab, which was working on the atomic bomb. Later, he became part owner of a company that designed and developed nuclear reactors for power generation.

Wilkins' achievement has been in the development of shields against gamma rays from the sun and nuclear sources. Wilkins developed the mathematical models by which the amount of gamma rays absorbed in a given material may be calculated. This technique is in wide use among researchers in space and nuclear projects.

Rufus Stokes

Inventor
1924-1986

Rufus Stokes' concern for cleaner air for all Americans caused him to focus his research on developing air-filtration equipment. Stokes was born in Alabama, and later moved to Illinois where he worked as a machinist for an incinerator company. In 1968, he was granted a patent on an air-purification device to reduce to a safe level the gases and ash from furnance and powerplant smoke. The filtered smoke became nearly invisible.

Stokes has tested and shown several models of his clean air machine in Chicago and others places. His system is intended not only to aid people with respiratory problems, but to benefit plants and animals as well. Another special effect of the filtered air is the improvement in the appearance and durability of objects such as, cars and buildings that are usually exposed to outdoor pollution over lengthy periods.

Dr. Jewel Plummer Cobb

Biologist, Physiologist
1924-

Dr Cobb has managed to pursue three careers—in science, education and administration—and achieve remarkable success in each. A graduate of Talladega College, Dr. Cobb earned her M.S. and Ph.D. in cell physiology from New York University. She is first and foremost a scientist,whose research has led to discoveries concerning normal and malignant pigment cells.

While fascinated by her work in cell physiology and cancer research, she has never been able to exclusively limit her energy to the laboratory. Dr. Cobb has remained committed to education, and has always left room in her schedule for direct contact with students. Her love of science has enabled her to spark her students' curiosity in biology, anatomy, research surgery and zoology. She has developed programs to reach out to minority students, and was a charter member of Connecticut's Committee for Minority Involvement in Higher Education. She has encouraged greater representation of women in science-related fields.

She was Dean of Douglass College, the women's division of New Jersey's Rutgers University, combining the top administrative post with holding high faculty rank in biological sciences. In 1981 Dr. Cobb's career was launched in a new direction with her assumption of the presidency of California State University at Fullerton. The recipient of numerous honorary degrees from colleges and universities. Dr Cobb also sits on the boards of directors of leading educational, public service, arts and business institutions.

Reprinted from: CIBA-GEIGY Corp. pamphlet "Exceptional Black Scientists"

Spencer Robinson

Spacecraft Engineer
1926-1968

Spencer Robinson, for most of his career, was an advance design engineer for McDonald-Douglass Aircraft Co. At his untimely death, president Lyndon B. Johnson cited him for "...devoted and selfless consecration to the service of our country...". This was the legacy left by Robinson to the African family of North America, as well as, to the United States. As a mechanical engineer, he went on to blaze new and daring trails in the space field.

In 1959 Robinson was involved as a supervisor in the Nike-Hercules, the Nike-Zeus and the Genie Missile programs. In 1964 Robinson became deputy director of manned space programs at McDonald-Douglass. He was another person of the African Family in North America who contributed to the United States Space Programs.

Virgil G. Trice, Jr.,

Chemical Engineer
1926-

Virgil Trice spent 30 years in developing nuclear energy and now is primarily concerned with managing the radioactive

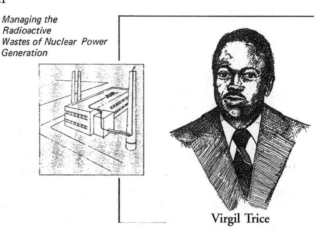

Managing the Radioactive Wastes of Nuclear Power Generation

Virgil Trice

waste resulting from nuclear power generation.

Trice had been working in the waste management field since 1971 when he joined the Atomic Energy Commission. He moved from the AEC., to the Energy Research and Development Administration, then to the Department of Energy. Trice is responsible for radioactive waste management planning, reporting, and program control; an area important to the future of nuclear power. From 1949 to 1971, Trice worked at the Argonne National Lab. In research and development, economic evaluation, and program planning of concepts for nuclear fuel reprocessing and power reactors.

Trice was born in Indianapolis, Indiana. He received his B.S. and M.S. degrees in chemical engineering from Purdue University. He also has a degree in Industrial Engineering from the Illinois Institute of Technology. His career includes teaching as an Associate Professor of Chemical Engineering at Howard University.

Richard B. Spikes

Inventor
DOB - unknown

Richard Spikes is credited with having a number of inventions. Many of his inventions have been recognized by some large corporations such as, the Milwaukee Brewing Company. One of his most famous inventions was the automatic safety brake system which was patented in 1962. He invented a brake combining the best of both hydraulic and electrical systems. Before he went blind, Spikes invented a drafting machine for the blind in order that he might finish his work.

Spikes is responsible for the following inventions:

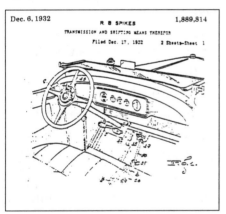

Outside view of modern transmission and shifting means therefor

The modern version of the Railroad Semaphore, in 1906. Automatic Car Washer and auto directional signals, in 1913 (Piece-Arrow). The beer-key tap, in 1910 (Milwaukee Brewing Co.). The continuous trolley pole for electric railways in 1919 (San Francisco "Key Line").

Patent # 1,59,0557, June 29, 1926: Combination milk/bottle opener.
Patent # 1,828,753, Oct. 27, 1931: Meth. & Apparatus etc.
Patent # 1,889,814, Dec. 6, 1932: Automatic gearshift
Patent # 1,936,996, Nov. 28, 1933: Transmission, and shifting thereof
Patent # not found, about 1910: Self-locking rack for billiard cues
Patent # not found, about 1939: Automatic Shoeshine chair that folds up
Patent # not found, about 1940: Multiple barrel machine gun

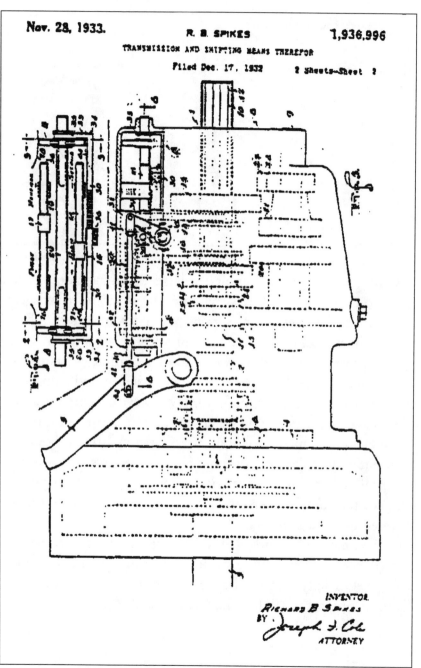

Nov. 28, 1933.

R. B. SPIKES

1,936,996

TRANSMISSION AND SHIFTING MEANS THEREFOR

Filed Dec. 17, 1932

2 Sheets-Sheet 2

INVENTOR.
Richard B Spikes
BY
Joseph J. Cole
ATTORNEY

Inside view of modern transmission and shifting means therefor

Meredith Gourdine

Physicist, Engineer
1929-1998

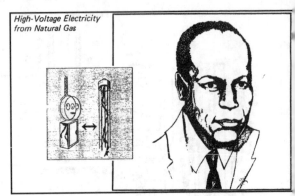
High-Voltage Electricity from Natural Gas

Meredith Gourdine

Meredith Gourdine was a recognized authority in the field of direct energy conversion. Gourdine pioneered work in electrogasdynamics, (EGD) a way of producing high-voltage electricity from natural gas. Gourdine's research has the potential to improve refrigeration for food preservation, supply power for heat and light in homes, burn coal more efficiently and de-salt sea water.

Meredith Gourdine was head of Gourdine Systems Inc., Research and Development firm of New Jersey, and along with his associates, have developed a variety of devices, they are as follows: An exhaust-purifying system for cars, equipment for reducing incinerator smoke-pollution from older apartment houses; a technique for dispersing fog from airport runways; and a system for production-static spray coating of metal products, which reduces production costs and limits the amount of pollutants released to the atmosphere.

Gourdine's Mark 1 high voltage generator converted kinetic energy in a flowing stream of compressed air into high voltage electricity without the use of turbines or rotary machines. Gourdine won the 1966 Industrial Research Award.

EGD DUST MONITOR

A unique application of the EGD principle has many uses in the monitoring of particulate matter in a gaseous medium.

When a gas containing particulate matter is passed through an ionizing section, we place a charge on the solid particles. If we now collect and store these charges, we have a high voltage power supply, or power generating station; if however, we short circuit the collector through an ammeter to ground, we have a virtually direct method of measuring the amount of particulate matter in the gas. The current flow through the meter is directly proportional to the number of particles which the systems handles.

A few of the applications of his system are:

Monitoring exhaust gases for pollution measurements;
Monitoring process plants for process conditions;
Monitoring atmospheres for excessive dust loading;
And many others...

EGD AUTOMOTIVE EXHAUST PRECIPITATION

Particulate matter, inherent to the exhaust of an internal combustion engine, is removed from automotive missions by EGD.

Precipitation of particulate matter is accomplished by passing the engine's exhaust flow through a venturi, where the particles are charged via a corona discharge. These charged particles are swept downstream from the venturi and are deposited on the walls of the collector. The deposition is caused by the mutual repulsion unipolar charge particles exhibit.

Physically the device consists of three components: (1) the venturi which serves as the source of ions, (2) the collector, and (3) the ion source power supply, all of which are labeled in the diagram.

It can be seen that only one electrode is at a high potential, and is not exposed and therefore, completely safe. The power necessary to operate the unit is less than 0.25 watts and its performance is not affected by temperature. This allows the unit to be placed at any position in the exhaust system. It should also be noted that the design of collector section is a removable insert which offers an attractive after-market.

WHAT IS EGD?

Basically, EGD, electrogasdynamics, is the exploiting of kinetic energy of gas stream to push along molecular ions from a region of low potential to one of high potential, where a collector can gather them. The physical principles are not new. What is new is the solving of problems of ion drift, space charges effects and useful concentration of power.

The molecular ions are easily inserted at the point of low potential by a corona discharge unit consisting of a corona electrode (a point) and an attractor electrode (an annular ring). The ions leave the corona point and head toward the attractor. The circuit would end there except that the gas stream seeps them beyond the attractor, toward the collector.

The force of the gas stream determines how far the ions can be pushed, and against what opposing potential. The opposing potential tends to send the ions back upstream (called ion slip). Another obstacle is the field potential of the ions themselves it makes them head for the walls of the tube.

EGD PRECIPITATION

The EGD technique is utilized to manufacture a particle precipitator. A corona discharge ion source is used to impart a uni-polar charge to the particulate products in the exhaust. The degree of charging obtained is a function of the ion geometry, particle size, gas, velocity, applied charging field and the dielectric properties of the particulate. To obtain efficient charging, the parameters of the ion source are optimized for each application.

The gas velocity through the systems is large compared to the drift velocity of charge particles in the applied field of ion source. This enables the particles to be transported into the collector region. The accumulation of space charge within the collector gives rise to axial and radial space charge fields.

The gas velocity through the collector is reduced by an increase in cross section so that particle drift velocities in the radial field become significant. The charged particulates are accelerated by the radial space charge toward the wall, where they give up charge to the collector and are precipitated from the flow.

EGD COATING

A small EGD generator has successfully been made for use in an electrostatic spray painting gun. The channel is mounted integrally with the gun and develops a maximum output of 75 kv when loaded by the corona current of the spray gun. Operation is achieved at 60 psi and 6 cfm.

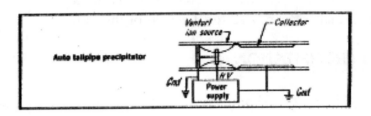

Voltage for the EGD ionizer is derived from a small, transistorized, battery-operated inverter which fits into the pocket of the spray gun operator. The batteries used are standard rechargeable flashlight cells. Overnight recharging is required occasionally, depending upon the actual duty cycle of the spray gun.

Irving W. Jones

Engineer
1930

Dr. Irving W. Jones, chairman and professor of civil engineering at Howard University, distinguished himself in his field. As a structural methods engineer, he used his expertise in designing and testing the structure and durability of spacecraft.

Dr. Jones did some of his work at Grumman Aerospace Corp., and at Fairchild-Hiller Corp. Some of his projects were the Lunar Excursion Module of the Apollo Vehicle, which landed on the moon. Here again are some of the creations of the African Family in North America in the 20th century.

Dr. Samuel Kountz

Physician
1930-1981

Dr. Samuel L. Kountz was born in Lexa, Arkansas on October 20, 1930. He received his elementary and college education in Arkansas. He graduated from the Agricultural, Mechanical and Normal College of Arkansas. He did graduate work at the same school earning a Master's degree in chemistry.

Following a competitive examination, he became the first black to be admitted to the University of Arkansas Medical School. It has been said that his interest in medicine stemmed from an incident when he was a young boy in Lexa, Arkansas. He accompanied an injured friend to a local hospital. Moved by the ability of doctors to ease his friend's suffering, he decided to become a physician. His father, a Baptist Minister, his mother and his grandmother, who had been born into slavery, encouraged him.

On completion of medical school, Dr. Kountz went to California where he interned at San Francisco General Hospital, and then spent six years in a surgical residency at Stanford University Medical Center. During his training at Stanford he became interested in kidney transplantation. He did animal experiments on kidney transplantation and how to avoid rejection by the recipients of kidneys. He discovered that large doses of the steroid drug, methylprednisolone could help reverse the acute rejection of a transplanted kidney. Other researchers took advantage of Dr. Kountz's observation and used similar large doses of the drug methylprednisolone in the treatment of many other conditions.

While at the University of California in 1967, he worked with other researchers to develop the prototype of a machine that is now able to preserve kidneys for up to 50 hours, from the time that they are removed from the donors' body. The machine is used worldwide and is named the Belzer Kidney Perfusion machine in honor of Dr. Kountz's partner, Dr. Folkert O. Belzer. He was also a member of the medical teams at the University of California at San Francisco and at Downstate Medical Center who advanced tissue typing tests to improve the results of kidney transplantation.

Dr. Kountz progressed academically to the rank of Professor of Surgery at the University of California, San Francisco School of Medicine. In 1972, after a national search, he was invited to become Professor and Chairman of the Department of Surgery at State University of New York, Downstate Medical Center in Brooklyn. In five years at this institute he performed over 500 kidney transplants, then believed to be the most in the world. What is of considerable interest here is that he performed these transplants regardless of the patients ability to pay. It has been found in the Harlem Community that one out of every three people has hypertension and that a number of these people will develop renal failure. Although Harlem Hospital Center has the ability to prolong life through renal and peritoneal dialysis, we look to renal trans-plantation, made more successful by Dr. Kountz, to enable patients to lead normal lives without the need to spend four or more hours on a machine, three times a week at the hospital.

Dr. Kountz was actively involved with many organiza-tions whose goals were to improve the quality of life for poor people through improved health care. When he became ill in

1977, in addition to being Director and Chairman at Downstate Medical Center, he was Surgeon-in-Chief at Kings County Hospital Center and President of the Empire State Medical Society, the state branch of the National Medical Association, which is made up primarily of black physicians.

Dr. Kountz has received many honors. He is a member of several honor societies. He holds honorary degrees from the University of San Francisco, University of Arkansas and Howard University.

Dr. Kountz has had inexhaustible energy. He belonged to some 37 societies in which he has been active in an effort to improve health care for all. Dr. Kountz had a great social conscience -and when he came to Brooklyn, he indicated that one of his very important reasons for moving to Brooklyn was to improve the quality of medical care for the black community. This he did working long hours and often not going home, but taking quick naps in his office.

Dr. Kountz has also improved the skills of other physicians. He has not only directly trained many physicians in his specialty, but has published 173 scientific papers to help physicians throughout the world with their skills.

We, at Harlem Hospital Center are proud to salute this great human being who did so much to revolutionize kidney transplantation which has not only benefited people throughout the world, but has prolonged life here in our Harlem community.

Dr. Kountz was rumored to have been considered a Nobel Laureate candidate 3 or more years prior to his death, 12/24/81. This covered the fields of chemistry, biochemistry, biophysics, and pharmacy.

Thanks must be rendered to Ms. Stella Gordon, Executive Assistant to the Harlem Hospital Center Community

Board, past and present board members for the New York Times article caption 12/24/81, and the Harlem Hospital Center Community Board Resume on the life of Dr. Samuel L. Kountz.

Physician Dr. Kountz was the grandson of slaves who rose to become one of the foremost surgeons of his time. As an international leader in organ transplantation surgery, he brought hope to hundreds of people who previously would have had little chance of survival.

Throughout his career, Dr. Kountz performed more than 500 kidney transplants and pioneered new techniques in preserving organs and reducing organ rejection.

Dr. Kountz's early schooling in rural Arkansas limited his access to a major university. He enrolled at Agricultural, Mechanical and Normal College of Arkansas, graduating third in his class there. Despite an early rejection from medical school, he was able to qualify by earning a master's degree in biochemistry from the University of Arkansas. He then became one of the first black students to enroll in the University of Arkansas Medical School. While a resident in surgery at the Stanford University Medical School, Dr. Kountz set up an organ transplant unit and did animal experiments on kidney transplantation and immunology.

After heading the kidney transplant program at the University of California at San Francisco for five years, he moved to New York to become head of surgery at the Downstate Medical Center and chief of general surgery at Kings County Hospital Center. Following a trip abroad in 1977, Dr. Kountz contracted an illness which left him brain-damaged and incapacitated for the rest of his life. He died an untimely death in December 1981 at the age of 51.

69

Dr. LaSalle D. Leffall, Jr.

Cancer Surgeon
1930-

Dr. Leffall is a surgeon, oncologist and medical educator who has received international recognition for his contributions to cancer research and surgery. He has served as professor of surgery and chairman of the Department Of Surgery at the Howard University College of Medicine since 1970. Dr. Leffall also was president of the American Cancer Society from 1978-1979.

Born in Tallahassee, Fla., Dr. Leffall was encouraged by his parents, both teachers, to pursue a medical career. He was valedictorian of his high school class and went on to receive his B.S. degree with greatest distinction from Florida A&M University. He was the ranking student in the 1952 class of the Howard University College of Medicine and president of the Kappa Pi honorary medical society.

Dr. Leffall spent two years as a senior fellow in cancer surgery at the prestigious Memorial Sloan-Kettering Cancer Center in New York City. Following medical service with the U.S. Army, he returned to Howard University in 1962 to begin his career as a surgeon and teacher. A compassionate, engaging and energetic man, Dr. Leffall is revered by his students, beloved by his patients and highly respected by his fellow surgeons.

Living up to his own description of surgeons as "people who know medicine and render service with genuine compassion," he also states that one of the highest standards of surgical discipline is "equanimity under duress." Dr. Leffall has taught and lectured at medical institutions around the world.

Reprinted from: CIBA-GEIGY Corp. pamphlet "Exceptional Black Scientists"

Annie Easley

Computer
Scientist
1933-

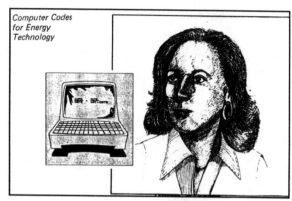

Computer Codes
for Energy
Technology

Annie Easley

Annie Easley was born in Birmingham, Alabama, on April 23, 1933. She is among a group of women who are making major contributions to energy research and management. Ms. Easley is engaged in research at NASA's Research Center in Cleveland, Ohio. She develops and implements computer codes used in solar, wind, and other energy projects.

Ms. Easley's energy assignments have included studies to determine the life of storage batteries (e.g., those used in electric vehicles) and to identify energy conversion systems that offer the greatest improvement over commercially available technology.

Easley while at NASA, and it's predecessor agency since 1955, continued her education in 1977. She obtained a degree in mathematics from Cleveland State University.

James Harris

Nuclear Chemist
1932-

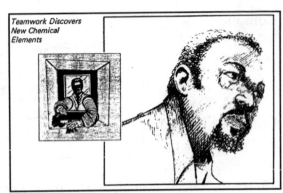

Teamwork Discovers
New Chemical
Elements

James Harris

Nuclear Chemist James Harris was a member of the scientific team at Lawrence Berkeley Laboratory that discovered two new elements just a few years ago. Harris joined the laboratory, which is operated for the Department of Energy by the University of California, in 1960 after years of research at Tracer Lab., Inc.. At Berkeley, Harris sought to complete the periodic table of chemical elements.

During the course of several years, this laboratory produced a number of new elements by bombarding special targets in an accelerator. The research team purified and prepared the target material and, after hundreds of hours of bombarding the target with carbon, element 104 was detected for a few seconds in 1969. Element 105 was produced in 1970, when the target was bombarded with nitrogen. Element 104 was named Rutherfordium, and 105, Hahnium, in honor of two atomic pioneers.

Harris unlike most of his colleagues didn't have a PhD. degree. The Texas born scientist had a B.S. from Houston-Tillottson College (A Black College) in Austin, Texas. Harris had taken graduate courses in chemistry and physics. Houston-Tillottson College conferred on him an honorary doctorate in 1973, largely because of Harris' work as co-discoverer of ele-

Delon Hampton

Civil Engineer
1933-

"If it has anything to do with under-the-ground, that's my business." Delon Hampton, a famous geotechnical engineer stated these words. Hampton emphasized that his specialty dealt with the composition of soil and rock. He also specialized in the design and structure of foundations, and structures beneath the ground such as: tunnels, earth dams, dams, viaducts, and bridges.

One of Hampton's accomplishments was for the Metropolitan Sanitary Department of Greater Chicago, Illinois. He designed a system of underground intercepting structures, connecting tunnels and sluice gates which have become a part of Chicago's reservoir and tunnel system. His finished work now regulates the supply of stored water into the city's water processing plants at a controlled rate.

Caldwell McCoy

Engineer
1933-1990

    As program manager for the National Magnetic Fusion Energy Computer Network, Caldwell McCoy directs the Nation's largest network devoted to a single scientific problem achieving usable energy from magnetic fusion. The Department of Energy network serves over 800 users of experimental data across the country.

    Caldwell McCoy was born in Hartford, Connecticut and he earned an electrical engineering degree at the University of Connecticut. McCoy continued to receive both master and doctor of science degrees. The latter in telecommunications from George Washington University.

    From 1959 to 1976 McCoy designed, tested, and evaluated systems for detecting and tracking submarines. For his achievement in developing long-range anti-submarine systems at the Naval Research Lab. in Washington, D. C., he was awarded the laboratorie's Thomas Edison Fellowship in 1968. In 1976 McCoy became a part of the magnetic fusion energy program; first with the Energy Research and Development Administration, and then, its successor agency, The Department of Energy.

Clarence L. Elder

Inventor
1935-

Clarence L. Elder is head of his own research and development firm in Baltimore, Maryland. He was awarded a patent in 1976 for a monitoring and control energy conservation system. Elder's "Occustat" is designed to reduce energy use in temporarily vacant homes and other buildings, and may be especially useful for schools and hotels. The system consists of connecting each energy unit to an electronic beam attached to the building entrance, to monitor incoming outgoing occupants. When the house or apartment is empty of people, the beam sets the Occustat system into motion reducing energy demand, achieving energy savings up to thirty six percent.

Elder and his associates also developed other systems for which they have received twelve U.S. and foreign patents trademarks and copyrights. Born in Georgia, Elder graduated from Morgan State College in Baltimore, Maryland.

Dr. Augustus A. White III

Physician
1936-

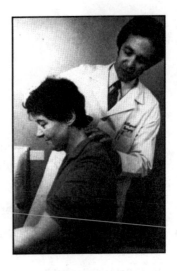

Dr. White is a scientist who has distinguished himself on many fronts, most notably orthopedics. He is orthopedic surgeon-in-chief at Beth Israel Hospital in Boston, Mass., and a full professor of orthopedic surgery at Harvard Medical School and the Harvard-MIT Division of Health Services and Technology. Dr. White's career goals shifted from psychiatry to orthopedics as a result of his experiences on the football team while an undergraduate at Brown University. A star athlete as well as a scholar, he became fascinated by orthopedic treatment of sports injuries, and went on to specialize in orthopaedic surgery as a medical student at Stanford University. Following graduation, his skills were further honored at the Karolinska Institute in Sweden, where he received his doctorate in medical science.

Dr. White is an avid researcher whose major efforts are directed at study of the spine and fracture healing. He has authored and collaborated on more than 100 scientific publications, books and articles. Most noted among them is the highly-regarded definitive work *"The Clinical Biomechanics of the Spine, and Your Aching Back: A Doctor's Guide to Relief."*

Dr. White is committed to helping students, and takes an active interest in their developing careers. He was one of the recipients of the United States Jaycees' Ten Outstanding Young Men Award, and the Martin Luther King, Jr., Medical Achievement Award. Dr. White is a member of Brown University's board of fellows. As a captain in the U.S. Army Medical Corps in Vietnam, he did extensive volunteer work in a leper colony.

Reprinted from: CIBA-GEIGY Corp. pamphlet "Exceptional Black Scientists"

Dr. Walter E. Massey

Theoretical Physicist, Educator
1938-

Dr. Massey is a theoretical physicist who has become a nationally recognized leader in scientific research administration. He has served as director of the Argonne National Laboratory and as professor of physics at the University of Chicago since 1979. In 1982 he was appointed vice president for research at the university.

The son of a school teacher and a laborer in Hattiesburg, Miss., he entered Morehouse College on a Ford Foundation fellowship at age 16. It was a turning point in his life because the educational experience changed his interest in mathematics into a love for physics. After graduating from Morehouse, he received his master's and doctorate degrees in physics from Washington University in St. Louis, Mo. Dr. Massey then conducted postdoctoral research at that university and at Argonne before taking teaching positions at the University of Illinois and at Brown University. Brown named him professor of physics and dean of the College at age 36. Dr. Massey is committed to bringing more minorities into science and to improving the quality of science education. He works hard, in groups such as the Society of Black Physicists, to make minority students more aware of role models in science and to help them discover the "joys of science." He is a trustee of Brown University, a board member of the American Association for the Advancement of Science, and a member of the National Science Board.

Reprinted from: CIBA-GEIGY Corp. pamphlet "Exceptional Black Scientists"

Carl English

Engineer
1938-

Carl English began his engineering career at RCA working first with large scale generalized computer systems using vacuum tubes; introducing to the world the first of it's kind. English in 1971 formed one of the earliest data terminal leasing companies which was independent of Western Electric and AT&T, known conventional carriers. He rose from national manager of field engineering in 1969 at Leasco Response, Inc., to Vice-President of Leasco Data Communications Corp. This subsidiary specialized in rapid message data communications to terminals throughout the world.

Dr. Reatha Clark King

Research Chemist, Educator
1938-

Dr. King is a chemist and educator who has been a pioneer in thermochemistry research and in university administration. Since 1977 she has served as president of Metropolitan State University in St. Paul, Minn. An innovator all her life, Dr. King has led Metropolitan State - a university without a central campus - to the role of "change agent" among educational institutions. During 1982-1983 Dr. King served as chairman of the board of the American Council on Education, a group which includes nearly every major college and university in the U.S.

Born in rural Pave, Ga., Dr. King had planned to return to her hometown after college to teach home economics, but was influenced by a professor to major in chemistry and go on to graduate school. After receiving her bachelor's degree in chemistry and mathematics from Clark College in Atlanta, Ga., she earned her master's and doctorate degrees in chemistry at the University of Chicago, where she was one of only two black graduate students at the time. Dr. King continued her research in high temperature chemistry at the National Bureau of Standards in Washington, D.C. for five years.

In 1968 she entered college teaching and administration at York College of the City University of New York, and later became professor of chemistry and associate dean for academic affairs. She received her MBA degree from Columbia University in 1977 just before assuming the presidency of Metropolitan State University. Dr. King is keenly interested in educational opportunities for women and minorities.

Reprinted from: CIBA-GEIGY Corp. pamphlet "Exceptional Black Scientists"

Cordell Reed

Nuclear Engineer
1938-

Cordell Reed, Ass't. Vice-President of the Commonwealth Edison Co. of Chicago, is in charge of nuclear licensing and environmental activities. Reed has been with the company since 1960, starting as an engineer assigned to the design, construction and operation of coal-fired generating stations. In 1967, he transferred to the nuclear division, with the task of developing more efficient and productive powerplants. Reed heads a group of seventy five engineers who were responsible for the engineering design of all nuclear projects.

Commonwealth Edison of Chicago became the nation's leading nuclear utility. Currently the company has seven nuclear powerplants in operation, capable of producing more than 5.4 mega kilowatts of electricity.

Reed, born in Chicago, Ill., holds a master's degree in engineering from the University of Illinois.

Donald Cotton

Chemist
1939-

Donald Cotton, the technical lead for nuclear chemistry research and development at the Department of Energy, plans, manages, and evaluates research and development on reactor materials and chemistry carried out in the agency's national laboratories. He identifies the breeder reactor needs of less - developed nations - an assignment which has taken him to several European states.

Dr. Cotton worked as a physical chemist at the Naval Propellant Plant at Indian Head, Md. From there, he moved to the Marine Engineering Lab., in Annapolis where he worked on the combustion of hydrocarbons as fuels and invented a microwave absorption technique measuring solid propellant burn rates. Cotton later researched liquid state chemistry and liquid propellants.

His career extended beyond the laboratory. Cotton was science editor for Libratterian Books, presenting scientific and technical subjects to lay readers.

Cotton has patents to his credit, and has written many scientific papers. Cotton's degrees in physical chemistry include an M.S. from Yale University and a Ph. D. from Howard University. Dr. Cotton has lectured at universities in Africa, and South America.

Ernest Coleman

Physicist
1942-1990

Ernest Coleman has directed high energy physics research at three Federal Agencies: The Atomic Energy Commission, The Energy Research and Development Administration, and The Department of Energy.

A Phi Beta Kappa student at the University of Michigan, Coleman received his B.S., M.S. and Ph.D. degrees there. He was awarded a year's research fellowship in high energy physics by the German Government and studied in Hamburg. Coleman returned to the U. S. and taught at the University of Minnesota, first as Assistant Professor of Physics and then as Associate Professor.

While serving as a visiting Professor at Stanford University, Coleman became director of the summer science program and has brought highly motivated and able students into the field of physics. Coleman received the Distinguished Service Award of the American Association of Physics Teachers.

Dr. Shirley Ann Jackson

Theoretical Physicist
1946-

Dr. Jackson is as intriguing and dynamic as the microscopic particles she studies. A native of Washington, D.C., she graduated valedictorian of her class at Roosevelt High School. From there she went on to the Massachusetts Institute of Technology and became the first American black woman to receive a Ph.D. from that prestigious university. Although accepted to do graduate work at Harvard, Brown and the University of Chicago, she decided to remain at MIT because she wanted to encourage the enrollment of more black students there. Dr. Jackson remains involved with the institution as a member of the MIT Corporation, the school's board of trustees.

Originally involved in high energy physics, Dr. Jackson now specializes in solid or condensed state physics. For two years, she was a research associate at the Fermi National Accelerator Laboratory in Batavia, Ill. She also served as a visiting scientist in the theoretical division at C.E.R.N. (European Organization for Nuclear Research), in Geneva, Switzerland. Dr. Jackson has written numerous articles for the leading physics journals and is a frequent speaker at scientific meetings.

She currently works at Bell Laboratories, the research anddevelopment arm of AT&T, where she works to expand the frontiers of knowledge in physics.

Reprinted from: CIBA-GEIGY Corp. pamphlet "Exceptional Black Scientists"

Dr. Jennie R. Patrick

Chemical Engineer
1949-

Dr. Patrick was the first black woman in the United States to earn a doctoral degree in chemical engineering. She credits her interest in learning to two of the best teachers she ever had, neither of whom attended school beyond the sixth grade. Those teachers were her parents, who advocated education as Dr. Patrick's ticket away from the hardships they had faced. After conducting research as a staff chemical engineer at the General Electric Company in Schenectady, N.Y., for several years, she currently is a senior research engineer at the Philip Morris Research Center in Richmond, Va.

Preparation for her scientific career began in a segregated school in rural Alabama. She studied at Tuskegee Institute and went on to receive a bachelor of science degree in chemical engineering from the University of California at Berkeley, and a doctoral degree in that field from the Massachusetts Institute of Technology.

Committed to the education of minority youth, Dr. Patrick travels the country encouraging high school and college students to pursue scientific and technical careers. Active on the National Council for Children and Television, Dr. Patrick is involved with developing television programs that depict positive role models of minority professionals working in technical areas. Dr. Patrick counsels young people to develop a firmly-defined self image, encouraging them "not to let others establish your potential."

Reprinted from: CIBA-GEIGY Corp. pamphlet "Exceptional Black Scientists"

Willie Hendrix

Inventor
1946-

Willie Hendrix, born on May 2, 1946, attended Pratt Institute in Brooklyn, New York and Howard University in Washington, DC. In 1980 and 1983, he developed and patented his invention, the Drixcle. Hendrix introduced his invention as:

The most advanced trike that money can buy! Drixcle is a new concept and improved three-wheel velocipede having a rear driving wheel and a pair of front steering wheels that can be pedaled forward and in reverse with relative ease,

• DEPENDABILITY: The frame is well engineered and strong, The trike is equipped with name brand parts.

• RIDING COMFORT: The cushioned seat and back support is without doubt one of the most comfortable seats ever designed for a trike. It also has a tool box below the seat.

• BETTER USE OF ENERGY: The rider can better utilize his energy more efficiently having the back as support it help relieves stress on arm and leg muscles.

• COMPACT AND LIGHTWEIGHT: The complete trike weights approximately 60 pounds. The overall length 86 inches long, width 36 inches and 40 inches high.

• SLEEK STYLING: Aerodynanic design greatly reduces wind resistance. The low center of gravty improves traction and maneuverabilty.

• PARTS INTERCHANGEARILITY: It is built with mostly standard 10 speed bike components and accessories. It can be serviced easily as most parts are available at our local bike shop .The Drixcle can be used, as an all purpose vehicle for exercise, transportation, and just for family fun.

• AFFORDABLE PRICES: The Drixcle is design for mass production and the price shall he within reach of the general public's purse.

Drixcle	Inventor
P.O. Box 627	Willie Hendrix
Nyack, NY 10960	Patent #4373740

Ronald E. McNair, Ph.D.

Physicist, Astronaut
(1950-1986)

Ronald McNair was famous as an astronaut, but he considered himself primarily a physicist-specializing in laser physics. He was also an accomplished jazz musician and held a fifth degree black belt in karate. McNair was born on October 21, 1950 in Lake City, South Carolina. He was an excellent student and athlete with a steadily growing confidence in his own ability to succeed. In 1967, McNair graduated from Carver High School in South Carolina. He continued his education and received his doctorate from MIT in 1976. Two years later Dr. McNair was selected as an astronaut candidate. After completing his training, Dr. McNair served as a mission specialist on Space Shuttle Mission 41-B in February 1984. With the completion of this flight, he had logged a total of 191 hours in space. "Keep your eyes on your goal. Don't let anybody tell you what you can't do," replied McNair when asked about his formula for success.

Dr. McNair was the second African American to travel in space. (Guion Bluford, Jr. was the first in 1983) He was mission specialist on the February 3, 1984, Challenger flight. McNair died in the space shuttle accident on January 28, 1986, when the Challenger exploded seventy three seconds after lift-off.

Billy T. Hervey

Flight Control Engineer

Born in Naples, Texas. Graduate of Prairie View A&M University.

Mr. Hervey joined NASA in 1964. Among previous assignments were those as Physical Science Technical Manager, NASA Flight Controller, Mission Control Center, Houston, Texas, for Gemini and Apollo flights, and Engineer, Kennedy Space Center, Florida. Awards include Group Achievement Award for support of Gemini missions; Group Acheivement Flight Operations Awards; Presidential Medal of Freedom Award for participation on Apollo 13 Mission Operations Team; and Johnson Space Center EEO Award.

THE BING GROUP

Dave Bing -- a retired pro basketball player, Hall of Famer, and founder and owner of The Bing Group. The group's automotive activities include: the assembly of car seats; the production of steel blanks; welded sections; and stamping services. The company sells its services to auto parts manufacturers and metal furniture and appliance makers. The

Dave Bing

Bing Group, considered to be one of the largest black-owned businesses in Michigan, consists of Bing Metals Group and Bing-Lear Manufacturing (a joint venture with Lear Corporation that manufactures automotive seats and adds color and detailing to bumpers).

WASHINGTON SENDS for DETROIT
By MARC CRAWFORD
Jet Magazine"

Joseph Blair

Into Washington, D. C.'s Pentagon one day last week hobbled balding, 54-year-old Joseph Blair, a Detroit hotel keeper whose arthritis was giving him "the devil." Minutes later, bypassing generals and admirals, the bespectacled grandfather was ushered into the office of the assistant secretary of defense for research and development, then to Building T, Room 2532.

Blair had been summoned to Washington to give the government some badly needed information on rocketry, which they had refused to accept for more than 30 years. Blair, a native of Augusta, Ga., who left Paine College after two years because he had no money, lectured to high officials, telling them why the Vanguard missile failed to put a satellite into orbit; how to put a rocket manned with human beings on the moon, then offered the government their choice of some 40 inventions—including rockets, submarines, ballistic missiles, guns and shells.

"Where have you been for the last 25 years?" one official un- wittingly asked. "Why haven't you come to us before?" Blair, said a witness, eyed the officials for a long minute, hung his head in embarrassment and muttered: "Sir, you know why—don't make me say it." The official flushed, there was a pause, and then the conference continued.

By the time Blair was ready to return to his small (26 rooms) hotel in Detroit, the Navy took three of his inventions for evaluation, stamped them secret and made a man, who had been laughed at all of his life, feel that his 38 years of trying had not been in vain.

"When I left that building," Blair recalled, "I was 10 feet tall. I felt for the first time in my life that I was an American. Not a colored American, but a plain American, you know what I mean?"

Blair shows model of hid "Batcraft", a highly maneuverable two-man submarine.

It meant a lot to Blair; more than money. This he proved in 1928 when the governmnent refused to consider a submarine, which Blair designed. France, Italy and Japan were interested in the futuristic craft, offered to buy it, "If the United States doesn't want it," Blair informed them, "then nobody in the world can have it."

Back in 1925 when Gen. Billy Mitchell was court-martialed for defying his superiors with his ideas on the value of air power, Blair, then in his native Augusta, recognized that the sky was a new frontier for modern warfare and by 1926 had built a 75mm anti-aircraft gun. Through the open door of the armory, he saw a 75-mm field piece and though he was not permitted near it, a kindly white man told him about the weapon.

Blair read all books on the 75 he could find, making the library his second home. Soon afterwards he built his gun. The barrel was fitted into a larger jacket which contained lights, much like sticking a pencil through a flashlight. When the light illuminated the target, the projectile in the center hit its mark.

Turning his attention to larger guns like the 16- and 21-inch coast defense rifles, Blair was disturbed because the shells would only travel 30 to 60 miles. He reasoned that the shell could go twice its range and even farther, if at the end of its normal range another charge would ignite, giving the shell new life and flight.

This discovery in 1928 led him to rockets in two stages

(the Jupiter-C Army rocket, developed last year, which placed the Explorer I satellite into outer space was a three-stage rocket). Blair offered his blue print to the government, but was rebuffed as he was to be again in World War II. Shortly after the Germans began their V-2 rocket attack against England in 1944, the harried inventor took his plans of the same type of rocket out of mothballs and offered them to

Blair and propellers he designed and manufactured.

the government. "They said it was fantastic and couldn't be done," Blair recalls.

Thirty years ago he had offered plans for aerial torpedoes and a plan for rocket launchers on submarine decks. During World War II, he was taken off of his crane operator's job at Ford Motor Co., and placed in the laboratory designing impellers (a sort of super-charger) for boats and aircraft. He developed the impeller for the P-47, the famed long-range American fighter-bomber.

And while he was making impellers for $1.40 per hour, he supplemented his income by making impellers for Horace

Dodge's racing boats. Even so, he continued to work with radar, which he became acquainted with in 1929.

Non-smoker, non-drinker Blair, who has never been to a tavern, has read thousands of books on science and engineering, but has never read a novel. Always, he says, he has been filled with the insatiable desire to know why things are and why they can't be improved. The why brought about the birth of dish-washing machines, mouse traps, aquaplanes and a compound called Blairite, which can withstand heat up to 3,500 degrees Fahrenheit. It also brought about Blair's "Batcraft," a two-man submersible torpedo boat, more maneuverable than a PT boat and much less expensive to manufacture. At one foot below water level, it can travel at 80 mph.

"In fact," Blair chuckles, "the most pressing question I haven't found an answer for is how to reduce from 212 pounds. I just like to eat too much I guess."

Those who used to laugh at Blair and call him a fool, now have found new respect for him, and said a former agitator: "Man, I tell you, our race can do anything."

As a result of his many jobs-well-done, it appears that the humble inventor is on the way to riches, but says he: "The most important thing to me is that some one has at last recognized the things I have given expression to. And about the money, if I get it, I'm going to use most of it on scholarships to deserving children. Not Negroes or whites, but American children. You know what I mean?"

HIS INVENTION KEEPS DRIVERS FROM SLEEPING

Wilbert Murdock

By SIMON ANEKWE
Amsterdam News Staff
2-7-84

Biomedical engineer Wilbert Murdock was just a small junior high school student when he had his dream.

He felt, indeed he was sure, he could become an Inventor and make life better for people. But he was equally certain at that time that he didn't know how to go about it.

So he nourished his dream as it drove him on to educational excellence and achievement, through private high school and Polytechnic University in Brooklyn and about a dozen other University courses in Brooklyn Polytechnic University.

He began there in 1975, but it wasn't until his junior year that he learned there was a way to fuse his interest in engineering and medicine.

"In my senior year I started taking bio-engineering courses and saw how my understanding of the human body could improve many aspects of human life," he said.

Long involved in athletics, Murdock had also studied

gymnastics and martial arts. In the Polytechnic classroom he "saw how the combined understanding of the human body from an athletic point of view, as well as, the medical, could help people."

"At that point I knew I could design a technology that no one else could design," he stated. He called it "KAD", Knee Alignment Device, describing it as:

"The first technology that will lead to a total solution for injury to the knee joint during athletic involvement. The U.S. KAD was issued last September and about a dozen other inventions are making their way to that office.

His inventions since he began working on KAD as an M.S. degree student are thus so many that it might seem the road has been easy. He had to quit his jobs teaching computer science at Baruch College, electrical engineering at NYC Technical College and general chemistry at New York University, so as to give all his attention to inventing.

At some point, "I lost everything, including my apartment. I had no income and life became extremely hard," he stated. But his parents, Karim and Rosa Murdock of the Bronx and close friends encouraged him on.

Giving up teaching, he started a company called Motiontronics for Science, with $30,000 from family and friends, he became its chairman and the only one working full time.. His associates' all bright young Blacks like himself, held other full time jobs.

KAD has "both preventive and rehabilitative" uses, he said. Worn over the knee, its sensors can detect any knee misalignments with a beep or voice. It can address knee alignment problems for the elderly and help with the design of better artificial limbs, Murdock explained.

The company's "at least a dozen other inventions" include

a device to keep drivers awake, an anti-collision device for cars, a laser system for dentistry, the budding engineer-businessman stated.

Now he would like to see the invention reach people who can use them. The company has built prototypes with that for KAD being tested at the State University of New York in Stony Brook.

Under-capitalized, Motiontronics for Science would like to go into joint venture with an established medical company to develop and market KAD and other inventions Murdock stated.

SHE GIVES SCIENCE BOOST

By CHRISENA COLEMAN
Daily News Staff Writer
4-25-96

Dr. Mae Jemison visited Harlem's Ralph Bunche School yesterday to launch a-new science program and encourage students to consider careers in science.

Dr. Mae Jemison

Jemison, a physician and chemical engineer, and the nation's first black female astronaut, conducted a series of hands-on experiments with electricity and ink to help the students understand that science can be fun.

"Children are natural scientists," said Jemison. "They are always trying to find out what the world is all about.... We must encourage them to use their. , . critical thinking skills and creativity."

Jemison said parents and students alike should get more involved with science because it affects every aspect of life.

"Science is everything, from administering medicine to a child, to the function of light bulbs," Jemison said. "There is a need for everyone to increase their science literacy."

New York Schools Chancellor Rudy Crew said the hands-on experiments were an excellent method of teaching science.

"When children learn science by actually doing it, they're developing the critical thinking, problem solving and team player skills that will serve them in all aspects of their lives," said Crew. "The future is information and technology-driven."

Jemison's visit to the Harlem elementary school was scheduled in conjunction with National Science and Technology Week.

Week.

Jemison joined Mildred Jones, director of the New York City Urban Systemic Initiative, in launching a new citywide hands-on science program.

"Our children's skills will improve if they have the opportunity to conduct the experiments, said Jones. This will stimulate the growth pattern, and hopefully it will produce more African-American scientists.

Jones said the students, most of whom are black or Hispanic, were surprised to see that Jemison was a young black woman.

"Based on what they see in their textbooks, all scientists are white men with bushy hair and white lab coats," said Jones. "It was awesome for them to see someone who looked like them..., It builds their self-esteem and gives them a can-do attitude."

JERSEY GENIUS INVENTS SOLAR HOT WATER SYSTEM THAT WORKS

By J. ZAMGBA BROWNE
Amsterdam News Staff
8-27-94

Professor Nedwell explains his solar hot water system.

Every Sunday, church folks hear how spiritual power comes from above. Now a local Jersey City professor and businessman, Kenneth K. Nedwell, has demonstrated that you can also tap into a physical source of the same power.

Professor Nedwell, a native of Antigua, invented his first solar hot water system back in 1981. Combining photo votalic cells with his system, he now can exact enough energy from the sun's-rays to heat and supply electricity to light your home and run its appliances: Proving the practicality of his invention, Nedwell points out that in 1991, the world market for oil was $13.50 a barrel. With today's prices already $31 per barrel, that is a 50 percent increase.

Nedwell, seeing the consumer need to meet these rising costs, plans to open an assembly line plant in Jersey City. His com- pany, UKAN Solar Enterprise, is already training ten students, who in turn will impart that knowledge to others on how to convert solar energy into electricity.

The students, all of whom are Black and Latino, are taught how to make solar collectors, assembly-blow units, electrical control systems, and liquid supply units. Classes are held Mondays through Fridays from 8 a.m. to 4:30 p.m.

Nedwell said the solar energy he produces is unpolluted,

inexpensive and features no hazardous waste. He invites consumers to look at the current cost for energy, add about 15 percent annually for a period of five years and they will agree that solar energy is the answer.

"With Black churches being deliberately overcharged by Con Edison for electricity," Nedwell continued, "solar energy will be the best bet, particularly for those religious institutions that can barely make it on their own."

Nedwell's long-range goal is to export his assembly plant to various countries, preferably South Africa and other Third World regions. "We will manufacture the necessary parts in the U.S and then sell the finished products abroad," he added. Professor Nedwell's invention is presently being used at two homes in Jersey City.

The solar power is supplied through a solar collector on the roofs of these Jersey City facilities. He explained that the function of the system is to focus the warmth of the sun and use it to heat a fluid container in a system of copper piping.

According to Nedwell the solar-heated liquid is then pumped into the hot water tank, transferring the warmth to the water, then circulated back up to the solar collector, reheated, and the cycle starts all over again.

During the days when the sun is inadequate to heat the water at night, professor Nedwell said the system will automatically switch back to gas and utilize the solar system whenever the sun's heat is enough to operate the water container.

Nedwell has already lined up a group of potential minority investors, including Blacks, Indians, Filipinos and Pakistanis. So far, Nedwell said he has spent in excess of $200,000 to perfect his invention.

After the system is produced at the factory or school, Nedell said it takes two men a full day to install it at a home. For detail about Nedwell's invention call (201)342-1080.

JOHNSON NAMED DEAN OF HOWARD UNIVERSITY SCHOOL OF ENGINEERING

Amsterdam News
7/6/96

Howard University president H. Patrick Swygert has announced the appointment af Dr. James H. Johnson Jr. as dean of the university's School of Engineering. The appointment was effective May 17, 1996.

Johnson is a professor of civil engineering at the school and has been serving as acting dean since 1995.

Swygert said, "Dr. James Johnson is a dedicated teacher, scholar and research scientist who has spent the last 25 years at Howard University working as a professor in the School of Engineering and as a professional engineer. Howard University is proud and fortunate to be able to select someone from its own ranks to provide the aggressive leadership necessary for the development of the vital research and educational roles of the School of Engineering."

Johnson joined the faculty of the Howard University Department of Civil Engineering in 1971 and has progressed through the ranks to achieve the rank of full professor. He has also served as chairman of the department from 1986 to 1994, as well as, interim vice president for research for the university in 1994. Since 1989 he has also been assistant director of the Great Lakes and Mid-Atlantic Hazardous Substance Research Center for the U.S. Environmental Protection Agency.

Over the years, Johnson has conducted extensive research in the areas of the re-use of wastewater treatment sludges and the treatment of hazardous substances. He has published more than 30 articles, contributed to one book and co-edited two books, including one on hazardous waste.

Additionally, Johnson has served as a consulting engineer on water treatment and sewer utility projects in the Washington, D.C. area, Florida, Livorno, Italy and Hartford County, Md.

Johnson has earned a bachelor of science degree in civil engineering from Howard University in 1969, a master of science degree in sanitary engineering from the University of Illinois, Champaign-Urbana, in 1970 and a Ph.D. in applied sciences from the University of Delaware in 1982. He is a registered professional engineer in the District of Columbia.

Howard University is the only comprehensive research university in the country that has a predominantly Black student population. It is a private insitution some 10,500 students enrolled in programs that encompass approximately 167 areas of academic concentration leading to bachelor's, master's and doctoral degrees, as well as professional degrees in law, medicine and dentistry. The university is ranked a Level I research institution by the Carnegie Foundation, one of only 88 such institutions in the country to be so designated.

Howard University is ranked first among all American colleges and universities in producing degrees conferred on African-Americans.

TWO SISTERS AGES 10 AND 8 INVENT BUG KILLING SPRAY

Amsterdam News
July 29, 1989

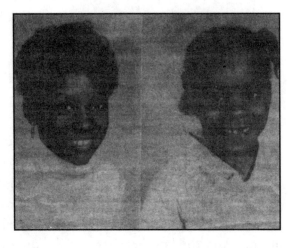

Two Harlem sisters ages 10 and 8 presently have an attorney working on a patent application for their invention, which they are already marketing.

The young inventors are Alicia and Miiya Bankhead, 10 and 8 years respectively. The elder sister will be in the fifth grade and the younger in the fourth, when P.S. 206 on 120th St. and Pleasant Ave., Manhattan, re-opens in September.

For three successive years, they have been Community School District Four Science Fair winners. It was their involvement in the science fair that led to the invention of what they call Poly-Pest Buster.

Their homemade PPB kills roaches, ants, termites and hornets like nothing else does, they said. Its efficacy was the chance discovery they made in their apartment. Later their father William Bankhead applied it "inside the crevices throughout the city housing complex."

The result, he said, was "no fleeing bugs:" Poly-Pest Buster did not give the bugs the chance to run. They were killed on the spot. With such a product, the inventors turned entrepreneurs and started selling the roach killer on 86th St. "Then we went down to the Village," the sister chimed during the Amsterdam News interview.

Asked how she got on to the path to invention, Alicia said it happened in the second grade and lost a weather chart. Her teacher had required her to trace the weather every day on the chart.

Their mother, Romaine went with her husband, William and Alicia to see the teacher. She agreed with Mr. Bankhead's suggestion that to compensate for the loss of the chart, Alicia would join the district science fair.

Alicia said the project in that first year, 1987, was "an acid and base test" for which she won both first and second prizes. She was given a microscope, a calculator and a trip to Albany.

In 1988 she did "a test on methane and Neil Bohl's law," Alicia said. Bohl, she eplained, "discovered the structure of the atom." And the law "teaches how he discovered the structure of the atom and how they trade places in the proton, electrons and the neutron," the fourth grader stated. She won second place.

By 1988 also the younger sister, Miiya, had joined the science fair. "By then I had already known Jack Perna, director of the science fair," she explained.

So as the elder sister worked on "methane and Neil Bohl's law," Miiya, in the second grade, did a project on "identifying steel and paper chromotography." Explaining what it was all about, she said "it is what doctors use to test for proteins and hemoglobin in blood."

Her first place award brought her a portable microscope, a solar pocket calculator and a trip to Albany. The district also recognized their father's encouragement to the two children and gave Miiya two science textbooks for her father. One was a hardcover to me.

Both children had been taking extra science lessons and doing projects at home with the help of their father. He is a Bronx Community College science major who, however, has done advanced work in chemistry beyond class requirements.

After going through the hard cover science textbook, Bankhead decided that Alicia and Miiya would work on slime as their 1989 science fair project.

They termed slime a "polymer" which has "two or more sensitive compounds with hydrogen bonding." They got an award for their joint project.

At home their dog likes the product and used to eat it all up. To stop that, they covered the slime with a chemical substance that the dog did not like, placed it on a plate and put it into a cabinet.

"Next day we found a lot of dead bugs" all around it in the cabinet, Alicia and Miiya stated. They could have shouted "Eureka," except that they were not really looking for that result.

No matter, they have their own roach killer: Poly-PestBuster. "There are three good things about it," Alicia stated. "First, it is thick and sticky. Placed in bugs' crevices and nests, it keeps bugs from coming out and starts to kill them immediately.

"Second, there is a compound in this polymer that causes it to evaporate, giving the time-release action. That means the molecules of the poison bust open faster in the summer and slower in the winter, making it effective for about a year.

"And third, when it dries to a hard cellophane plastic, it seals up holes and crevices and still kills," the proud young scientists explained.

DR. JUSTICE LEADS FIGHT AGAINST AIDS IN BLACK COMMUNITY

The Final Call June 15, 1992
by Richard Muhammad
East Coast Correspondent

NEW YORK—Dr. Barbara Justice's search for a tangible way to help Black people took her out of a career in teacher to medical school and eventually to Africa,

A cancer surgeon by training, she was the first Black doctor to seek and use the Kenyan-developed AIDS treatment Kemron to help Black AIDS victims. Kemron and Immunex' are non- toxic, alpha-interferon treatments, taken in pill form by AIDS patients.

A City College of New York alumna, she taught public school before attending medical school at Howard University. She graduated in 1977, spent five years in general surgery at Harlem Hospital, returned to Howard for special training in cancer surgery, then returned home.

A native New Yorker, with dreadlocks and a deep, dark chocolate-colored complexion, she works behind a desk of well-organized clutter: books, papers, charts and folders. Awards and pictures surround her on office walls.

For over two years, Dr. Justice has fought against AIDS in the Black community. In an interview at the Harlem brownstone, which is her home and office, she shared a wide range of AIDS information.

"There is no physician practicing in an urban area with African people that is not seeing AIDS, and has not been seeing increasing numbers of people afflicted since the beginning of the 1980s," stated Dr. Justice. She believes she saw her first AIDS patients at Harlem Hospital in 1979. Three patients died quickly from tuberculosis and medication didn't help them, she recalls.

As AIDS spread in the early 1980s, it concerned her and other Black doctors and by the mid-80 they were sponsoring lectures and AIDS forums.

But a health program she does over radio station WLIB led her to Kemron and treating AIDS patients when she and morning talk show host Imhotep Gary Byrd shared an article about Kemron.

They searched for more information, found little and journeyed to Nairobi, Kenya with a camera crew to record President Daniel Arap Moi's announcement of Kenyan success with Kemron in July, 1990.

She met Dr. Davey Koech, director of the Kenya Medical Research Institute which developed Kemron, and attended a symposium.

Scientists from the world over, except the U.S., listened to Kenyan data on patient improvement and findings that some patients became HIV-negative and had a rise in T-cell counts, she noted.

The reported rise in T-cell counts and patients becoming HIV negative has helped create controversy because no one has duplicated those results, she explained.

But, Dr. Justice added, "The most important thing they reported in my opinion was that the patients were getting better." She disagrees with a recent Department of Health and Human Services report that Kemron doesn't work. FDA's conclusions were partly based on some reports, old and invalid, in which Kemron was taken improperly or unstable medication was used, she said.

The best way to assess Kemron, or Immunex, is in clinical trials, she said. Clinical trials allow patients to receive the drug cheaply as medical investigators track their progress.

The problem is that decisions about clinical trials are tainted, she charged. Research is driven by demands for cures, big money pharmaceutical companies and whether research on prospective treatments is being done by investigators, Dr. Justice said.

On her initial trip, Dr. Justice stayed weeks in Kenya, visiting hospitals, making rounds, initiating treatments, watching patient progress. She went back and forth to Kenya before accepting patients.

When fighting over who developed and would benefit financially from Kemron and Immunex blocked exportation of the treatments, she started organizing trips for 72 patients to go to Kenya for help.

But news of Kemron's success has meant pain. A white newspaper accused Dr. Justice of denying treatment to Cedric Sandiford, a survivor of the 1987 vicious racial attack in Howard Beach, because he didn't have money. Dr. Justice says she had treated Mr. Sandiford for free since the Howard Beach incident. He stopped coming after his last trip to Kenya, she said.

She had advised him not to go to Kenya in 1991 and wanted the trip restricted to research. Working with other organizers, Mr. Sandiford went anyway. After his death last year, New York newspapers ran articles about AIDS patients being "trafficked" to Kenya.

"I ended up in conflict with people who got involved that just saw this as a money making ordeal," she said, "I felt this was a medical and health issue. The sensationalizing of it did more harm than good."

Medical professionals still question Kemron's effectiveness because of the publicity, she added. She said she has had her house broken into, received death threats and has been followed.

The summer of 1991 brought a "blessing," she said. She met Dr. Abdul Alim Muhammad (now Nation of Islam Minister of Health) and former *Final Call* editor-in-chief Abdul Wali Muhammad in Nairobi.

The trio met with Dr. Koech, the *Final Call* did a cover story and Dr. Justice and Dr. Muhammad formed a coalition to provide Immunex as an alternative treatment for AIDS patients. (The Nation of Islam will soon exclusively distribute Immunex, under the tradename Immuviron, in the U.S.)

Dr. Justice treats several hundred patients with Immunex, in a nutritional, emotional, spiritual, vitamin, herbal and exercise program. "We don't call it a cure. We're calling It a treatment. I've only been using it for a year-and-a-half. So we don't know the long range effects," she cautions.

But her success has made her oppose AIDS strategies obsessed with condom distribution and needle exchange. She advocates widespread testing to either negative HIV or get help when HIV positive, "We need to emphasize that those who are going to survive into the 21st century are those who are quite prudent at this point," she said.

AIDS in America first became well known among homosexuals, "They set up certain guidelines based on their experience with the world. . .not necessarily the best guidelines for African people, Dr. Justice said.

Blacks need to hear about testing, virginity and guidelines for monogamy, polygamy, celibacy, mate-seeking and parenting, said Dr. Justice. "AIDS victims need support and we must develop our own solutions," she added, Conferences, wards and think tanks on changing behavior are needed, she said.

'There have been no conclusive studies that show there is a benefit in reducing HIV spread by giving out needles," Dr. Justice charged, warning sharing needles for "camaraderie" won't stop. Needle exchange promotes treatment, why not simply offer more treatment? she asks.

"The confusion that besets our people is enhanced by confused leadership," said Dr. Justice, explaining that initially New York Mayor David Dinkins was against needle exchange but with funding and state approval he flip-flopped.

Dr. Justice also believes AIDS is a weapon of genocide against Blacks. Cases among new intravenous drug users and homosexuals are dropping, she noted.

"We're talking about Black heterosexuals between age 15 and 50 being affected worldwide. If the whole world has not mobilized to stop it, it is genocide wherever it came from."

KENYAN SCIENTIST MAKES HISTORICAL AIDS TREATMENT BREAKTHROUGH

By William Pruitt

On July 27, 1990, the President of Kenya, Daniel Arap Moi announced that the drug KEMRON which was produced by the Kenyan Medical Research Institute.

(Kemri) along with the Kenya Agricultural Research Institute had completely cured 50 Aids Patients. However, with this historical announcement by the President of Kenya, the white owned press all but totally ignored it and it got limited coverage by the African American Press. To add validity to this finding, a delegation of responsible and competent African Americans that included popular WLIB Talk Show Host and Broadcast journalist Imhotep Gary Byrd,

Dr. Barbara Justice, M.D. Minister Clemson Brown of Trans Atlantic Production plus two Aids Patients, Mr. Cedric Sandiford, a victim of the Howard Beach racial attack and Ms. Effie Harvey of Queens, N.Y. was part of the fact finding group who journeyed to Kenya to gather first-hand information on this Historical Discovery.

From a Historical view, here is how Dr. Davy Koech of Kenya claim that Kemri (Kenyan Medical Research Institute) got started. Kemri was established in 1979. It started with only a few staff members and a small amount of facilities. From 1979 to 1989, the institute grew into a top medical research body in Africa, employing more than 1000 people. Dr. Koech said the first 10 years were tough and that they operated the first two years on borrowed premises and without an operation budget. They didn't have an address. They had to use Professor Mugambiz's private box for their official mail. (He was the second Director of Kemri and one of its first two scientists). During those first few years they did not have an account for their first Research Grant of S72,000 that they received from an International Funding Agency.

The institute grew because the Kenyan Government was very supportive, plus they received support from multilateral and bilateral donor agencies, foreign governments, and the goodwill of other organizations that they collaborated with, plus people of Kenya in general have started to appreciate the role of research in all phases of life.

Some of the achievements of Kemri before this Aids breakthrough was in the past few years, they generated operationally useful findings that have been implemented by the Ministry of Health in almost all areas of their operation. Some of their work have been recommended for use worldwide by the World Health Organization. They also developed a viable infrastructure in terms of personnel and facilities that is capable of handling Biomedical Research at any level. This gives them the capability to respond to any health problem. They are on the map world wide in terms of Biomedical Research.

Kemri gets most of its budget operation from the Kenyan Government and they solicit the rest of the money from various multilateral and bilateral donor agencies, Foreign Governments and other funding bodies. Some of the future plans for Kemri after the Aids treatment have been perfected is to redefine their priorities again to keep up with the times.

Reprinted from: "The American Black Male" September 1990

SOME CLAIMS THAT HAVE BEEN MADE ABOUT THE USE OF KEMRON

On December , 1989, the preliminary result of treating people with Aids with Kemron were mentioned by Dr. Koech at the tenth anniversary of Kemri. This resulted in some sensational headlines and mocking cartoons in local newspaper along with local herbalist who were claiming credit for Kemron's development. But in February 1990, Dr. Koech held an audience spellbound for more than 90 minutes as he made the official announcement about Kemron apparent efficiency in treating Aids. In that meeting, Dr. Koech described the hard solid scientific work and the lucky breaks that resulted in the development of Kemron. He spoke of a chance meeting with his soon to be collaborator, Dr Arthur Obel. The difficulty in determining an effective and non-toxic dose of oral IFN-alpha, and the various formulations of the drug that were tried before the current one, a lactose wafer, was found to be most effective. Some of the technical problems, Dr. Koech pointed out are due to the lack of sophisticated research equipment available in Kenya.

Dr. Koech displayed data which showed the rapid disappearance of eight symptoms of AIDS in 101 patients. Over a two to six-week period of treatment with Kemron, fatigue/weakness, appetite/weight loss, diarrhea, fever, mouth sores/ulcers/thrush, other infections (such as pneumonia) lymphadenopathy, and skin rashes completely disappeared in all but two of the 101 patients. At the end of the six weeks, only one patient still experienced fatigue/weakness, and only one still had diarrhea; all other symptoms had disappeared in these two. All eight symptoms disappeared in the other 99 patients, usually within the first two weeks of treatment.

A Voracious appetite and a dramatic increase in libidi

nous desire were reported as the predominant side effects observed by Obel, who spoke after Koech at the February conference.

Obel described Aids patients who had been brought to him, some of them on the verge of death, but who recovered their weight and lost the symptoms of the disease such as diarrhea, Kaposi' S sarcoma, herpes zoster, mouth thrush, and other opportunistic infections that are associated with Aids after treatment with Kemron. Besides the patients on the clinical trial, Obel says he has treated scores of other patients, a number of them from neighboring countries, and achieved similar results; Some 20 patients have even converted from sero-positive to sero-negative, this indicating the possible disappearance of the AIDS virus (HIV) from the blood after several weeks of therapy.

Dr. Koech and Obel are unable to explain exactly how or why Kemron works aside from the well-documented anti-viral properties of IFN-alpha,

THE RETURN OF THE AFRICAN AMERICAN DELEGATION

For two weeks Imhotep Gary Byrd, Dr. Barbara Justice and Minister Clemson Brown were in Kenya observing the result of the Kemron treatment of people suffering with the AIDS virus plus getting some historical background on Kemri.

When they returned on about August 12, Imhotep Gary Byrd announced that a live Press Conference would be held on his radio talk show from August 13 through August 16 so he and his fact finding group could explain their findings publicly and on radio for those who might be interested. Some of their findings, according to Dr. Barbara Justice, were that over 1200 AIDS patients had been treated with the drug Kemron. All of them have shown improvement. In fact, about 10% of those treated went from testing positive for AIDS antibodies and the AIDS virus itself disappeared from the patient. Also Kemron has been successfully used on patients in Texas and Japan.

Gary Byrd brought back with him documented video coverage of the trip highlights. Interviews with principals of the project and in depth medical reports were features on the Gary Byrd Show. Since then, Byrd and Dr. Barbara Justice have appeared on some local television shows and have been available for interviews for Press People.

It should be remembered that not only did the white owned press in America ignored this great medical breakthrough but when a Press conference was held by Dr. Koech following the scientific presentation during which questions were answered about production and commercialization of the drug, there were only two journalists from the Nairobi-Based International Press Corp, the largest on the Continent outside South Africa. This attitude only confirms what Kenyans and other Africans have known for a long time is the refusal of many Westerners to take seriously anything of a scientific nature coming out of Africa. It was also noted that the Western Journalists were the biggest skeptics when Dr. Koech made the reference to the drug last December, 1989. The foreign press dismissed as a non-event, the announcement of what must rate as one of the greatest break-throughs in the world-wide war against Aids. However, Dr. Koech knows that had this announcement been made in any other country occupied with non-Africans, there would have been Pandemonium.

SUPPORT GROWS FOR MATHEMATICIAN GABRIEL OYIBO

Starting in January of 1999 OTP ran a three-month series of far-ranging interviews with mathematician, Dr. Gabriel Oyibo. Professor Oyibo was the first to mathematically generalize and prove Einstein's theory of relativity, in an article entitled Generalized Mathematical Proof of Einstein's Theory Using A New Group Theory".

The professor also presented his Unified Field Theory. Because OTP is not a science journal, there was some who questioned whether or not Dr. Oyibo is "for real".

We offer the following from reknown Mathematician Eugene Brunelle, to help clear any concern.

General Critique Of Gabriel Oyibo's Research Work
By Eugene Brunelle, Sc. D, MIT
Member ASMF, AIAA, Am. ACad. Mechs. SIAM, AMS
Former Princeton University Professor

Reprinted from: "Our Time Press" August 2000

AFFINE TRANSFORMATION: LORENTZ TRANSFORMATION

It is important to view the contribution of Gabriel Oyibo in the following light: the knowledge base and technology base (especially, no computer technology was required to formulate the works) necessary to reproduce Gabriel's work have been in existence since 1915 for the relativistic work and since around 1890 for the classical mechanics work. From those time periods until the present ANYBODY and the same chance to present as Gabriel, but NO-ONE WAS CLEVER ENOUGH TO DO SO. Said differently, these works should have already been in the literature in sufficiently creative and developed minds existed in the time periods mentioned above; quite obviously it seems that they were not, as history confirms. Collaterally, a little reflection recalls that many noble works were the result of previously established works to allow the new discoveries to be made possible. Thus the work of Gabriel Oyibo have an extra patina of brilliance not often seen in previous opera magna, because he had the ability to see general patterns and general relations from specific relations that were complete un-apparent to the best of the previous contributors to this area of knowledge.

Reprinted from: "Our Times Press," August 2000

BREADTH OF APPLICATION: NON-RELATIVISTIC

A wealth of insights is available for any equation/coupled equations, linear or non-linear by using art combinations of newly recognize group theory principles and the affine transformation principles long know but little used and little understood in the literature (and principally for highly focused work on a particular subset of problems; e.g. composite plate theory) and not very carefully at times (in many instances). Simple but useful, people will be horrified at missing the concept or that their heroes missed the concept. Any equation can be written in any coordinate system, and in fact, any affine [fake] coordinate system.

Reprinted from: "Our Times Press," August 2000

BLACK PHYSICIST DIES; PRIZED DISCOVERIES PROPELLED U.S. INTO SPACE RACE

Amsterdam News
4/4/95
By Cathy Connors

Dr Walter S. McAfee, the African American physicist who discovered the mathematical calculations enabling radio signals to bounce off the surface of the moon, thus ushering in the era of interstellar space exploration, satellite communications and missile guidance systems, was buried in Asbury Park, N.J., last week.

For his work in physics, McAfee received the highest honors in his field and was recognized by President Eisenhower in 1956, who presented him with one of the first research fellowships from the secretary of the Army for post-doctoral studies at Harvard University and at laboratories in Europe and Australia.

McAfee, 80, was born in Ore City, Tex., in 1914 to Luther Franklin and Susie A. McAfee. He attended public schools in Marshall, Tex., graduating from high school with honors in 1930, subsequently earning a bachelor of science degree in mathematics (magna cum laude) fromWiley College in 1934. He earned a master of science in physics from Ohio State University in 1937 and a doctorate in physics from Cornell University in 1949.

Introduced to physics in high school, he discovered the work of Albert Einstein and wanted to get involved, he said in a

1985 interview. Because of discrimination, he was unable to find employment in electronics to help finance his college education.

His career took a circuitous route to his signifcant discoveries. He taught high school mathematics and science in Colum- bus, Ohio, and in 1942 was hired as a mathematical physicist for the Fort Monmouth Signal Corps, where he remained for 42 years and held a number of supervisory positions, retiring as scientific advisor to the U.S. Army Electronics Research and Development Command. He also served as director of scientific study and surveillance and target acquisition for NATO.

IT'S THE ONES WE DON'T HEAR ABOUT WHO ARE THE GREATS

by Betty DeRamus/ Detroit News

If you've never heard of inventor **Claude Harvard,** (who died recently in Harper Hospital, I'm not surprised.

If he had choked a coach, showed up in a wedding dress to marry himself, fathered children by six or seven women whose names he could barely remember, or allegedly urinated in front of some restaurant patrons, you'd know all about Claude Harvard.

But the 18-year-old Highland Parker never slam-dunked or stuffed the ball on a basketball court or caught a Hail Mary pass with seconds to score. He never gunned down anybody with a bullet-spitting Uzi, either.

He was just the genius behind some of the Ford Motor Co.'s manufacturing success. In all, the company patented 29 of Harvard's inventions.

The odds against becoming a black inventor in the 1930s were even higher than the odds against becoming a superstar athlete today.

After graduating from Henry Ford Trade School, Harvard was denied the journeyman's card all other graduates received. After filling out repeated applications for the card, he finally learned that it had been thrown into the trash can.

But the light of his genius caught auto pioneer Henry Ford's eye, and Ford Motor Co. made a place for Harvard. In 1934, Harvard, then 23, developed his most celebrated invention, a machine to find and reject faulty piston pins. Henry Ford himself sent Harvard to the 1934 World's Fair in Chicago to exhibit this invention.

A hotel that initially didn't want to give the inventor a room relented after discovering Ford had made the reservation.

"Soon word got around that a black man was displaying an invention for Ford, and all the blacks would pass by to get a look," Harvard said in a 1986 newspaper interview. Ford later sent Harvard to Alabama's Tuskegee Institute to showcase the machine. There, he struck up a friendship with famed scientist Dr. George Washington Carver and became the link between Carver and Ford.

When Carver asked for Harvard while attending a chemical convention in Detroit, Ford sent his personal plainclothes officers to find the inventor at an eastside bowling alley. That's how Harvard wound up attending a banquet with Ford and Carver in his "Brown Bombers" bowling shirt. Harvard left Ford in 1938 and eventually became an engineer for the U.S. Tank Automotive Command, retiring in 1977. In his later years, he taught blueprint reading to enrollees in a machinist training program sponsored by Focus:HOPE.

Shortly before Harvard's June death, Henry Ford Community College hosted a special tribute for him. The inventor was too ill to attend, but his granddaughter Mursalata Muhammad, showed up to accept the journeyman's card Harvard once had been denied.

"Claude understood what happened to him, but he was a man who was not bitter," says Thomas Armstead, assistant director of Focus:HOPE.

"He felt happy to have accomplished all the things he accomplished. One of his most important traits was his eagerness to share his knowledge — which was quite vast — with young men and women in his field."

Unity – James Sepyo

His own Tool & Die Company (1934 - 36) was doing well until the all white employees found out Claude was a black man. Events then turned for the worst.

BLACK MANUFACTURERS CONTINUE TO MAKE AN IMPACT

DAILY CHALLENGE TUESDAY, APRIL 7, 1998
By John William Templeton

A lot of uninformed commentators like to say "Black people are just consumers, they don't make anything." That's not true and has never been so. But when young people hear it often enough, they don't put manufacturing or engineering at the top of their career list.

So a young Black male student from San Jose State University studying for a engineering degree in mechatronics was very happy to have the opportunity to meet in person Boy E. Clay Sr., the "godfather" of Black Silicon Valley and one of the obstetricians that delivered the computer age.

Clay spoke as a Sunnyvale based company, Envirotest Inc., headed by Chester Davenport, topped the American Stock Exchange because of its announcement of a remote sensor system for detecting automotive emissions to be test-marketed by the City of New York.

Not only is envirotest (ENR:AMEX) a Black- controlled public company that is the leader in providing automotive emissions testing for states and localities, but another Black innovator in Houston, Meredith Gourdine, holds patents for devices to measure pollution.

Clay's products touch every American household and many more around the world. Every consumer electronic product sold in the U.S. is tested for electrical shorts on one of the hi pot (dielectric withstand) testers that his 20-year-old Company, Rod-L electronics of Menlo Park, makes. Rod-L's products are the only ones certified by the Underwriters Laboratory.

Ironically, in 1951, Clay was told by McDonnell Aircraft that "we have no jobs for professional Negroes" after receiving his mathematics degree from St. Louis University. Five years later he returned to become the programmer for McDonnell's first computer. By 1961, he was helping to write languages like Basic, Fortran and Cobol for Control Data.

In 1965, David Packard and William Hewlett recruited Clay to begin the computer operation for Hewlett-Packard Co. in Palo Alto, despite all the engineering talent surrounding them at their alma mater, Stanford University.

"I was the first employee of the computer operation and it literally grew under me," recalled Clay during: the first of the chat with Black Innovators series at the Tech Museum of Innovation in San Jose. His direct supervisor was Tom Perkins. "Tom went on to be the real founder of the venture capital industry and without venture capital, there would have been no personal computers because the large companies would not have taken the risk."

Clay had a personal example. "The Holiday Inn came to us and wanted a point-of-sale system, but they said, 'It can't fail,' so we built the first 'fault-tolerant' computer and were about to ship it to them, but Bill Hewlett called and said, "Cancel the order, we don't want to be in that business."

After Perkins left H-P to found Kleiner Perkins Caufield and Byers, the venture capital firm that funded 40 percent of the companies that have emerged in Silicon Valley. Clay also left six months later when passed over to take Perkins' job on a permanent basis. "My wife told me that if you work as hard for yourself as you have for other people, you'll be successful in anything you do."

Clay advised Perkins to put money into a new company to make the 'fault tolerant' computers, now the backbone banks, retailers, stock exchanges and other 24-hour applications. That company was Tandem Computers. He also consulted with Robert Noyce, the co-inventor of the transistor, who was trying to form a company called Intel 'There were so many things you could use these chips in that I suggested, "Don't try to make anything with them, just sell the chips."

And when a former Texas Instrumments engineer came calling for a new company to make personal computers, Clay also "greenlighted" Compaq for venture funding.

The savvy technologist also saw an opportunity for himself. Texas Instruments had dropped its personal computers after a highly-publicized series of fires caused by electrical shorts. The fledgling industry was in jeopardy of collapse. Clay devised a way to conduct the dielectric with-stand tests on the production line, rather than at the design stage, to insure that every machine wassafe.

William Hunter Dammond

Inventor

A Black U.S. Citizen, developed, and invented the Automatic Block Signal. The signal that one sees when travelling on subway trains which change from green to red, and red to green light. The purpose of this signal is to prevent a second train from following the preceding (first) train too closely for public safety. It became a vital part of mass-transportation in urban areas. The electrical circuit used ot operate these signals is called the "Dammond Circuit". William Hunter Dammond, of the African Family in The U.S.A., North America, invented this signal.

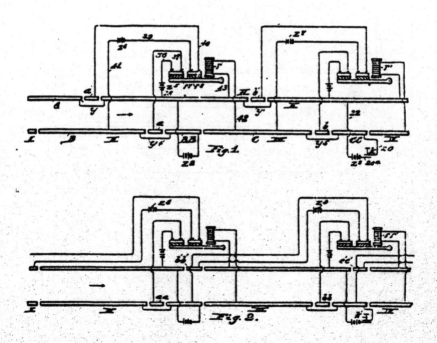

W. H. DAMMOND.
SAFETY SYSTEM FOR OPERATING RAILROADS.
APPLICATION FILED FEB. 17, 1905.

2 SHEETS—SHEET 2.

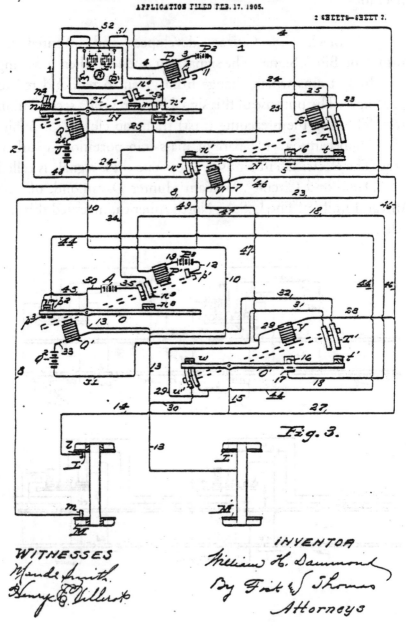

Fig. 3.

WITNESSES

INVENTOR

William H. Dammond
By Fit & Thomas
Attorneys

128

Elegant Woman - Abdullah Aziz   courtesy Grinnell Gallery

ACTIVISTS CHALLENGE CORPORATIONS THAT THEY SAY ARE TIED TO SLAVERY; TEAM OF LEGAL AND ACADEMIC STARS PUSHES FOR APOLOGIES AND REPARATIONS

By James Cox
USA TODAY
2-21-2002

They owned, rented or insured slaves. Loaned money to plantation owners. Helped hunt down the runaways.

Deadra Farmer-Paellmann

Some of America's most respected companies have slavery in their pasts. Now, 137 years after the final shots of the Civil War, will there be a reckoning? A powerhouse team of African-American legal and academic stars is getting ready to sue companies it says profited from slavery before 1865. Initially, the group's aim is to use lawsuits and the threat of litigation to squeeze apologies and financial settlements from dozens of corporations. Ultimately, it hopes to gain momentum for a national apology and a massive reparations payout by Congress to African-Americans. Neither goal will be easily achieved.

There is considerable evidence that proud names in finance, banking, insurance, transportation, manufacturing, publishing and other industries are linked to slavery. Many of those same companies are today among the most aggressive at hiring and promoting African-Americans, marketing to black consumers and giving to black causes.

So far, the reparations legal team has publicly identified five companies it says have slave ties: insurers Aetna, New York Life and AIG and fnancial giants J.P. Morgan Chase Manhattan

Bank and FleetBoston Financial Group.

Independently, USA TODAY has found documentation tying several others to slavery:
* Investment banks Brown Bros. Harriman and Lehman Bros.
* Railroads Norfolk Southern, CSX, Union Pacific and
    Canadian National.
* Textile maker WestPoint Stevens.
* Newspaper publishers Knight Ridder, Tribune, Media General, Advance Publications, E.W. Scripps and Gannett, parent and publisher of USA TODAY.

Successive generations of African-Americans, starting with slaves freed in 1865, have failed to persuade Congress to apologize and make restitution for slavery. Attempts by descendants of slaves to sue the federal government for damages have been dismissed.

• By targeting corporations, the activists are opening a new chapter in black America's quest to be compensated for 2 1/2 centuries of bondage. The activists contend that major corporations today possess wealth that was created by slaves or at the expense of slaves - and that it's time for African-Americans to reclaim that wealth.

Evidence against corporations sits in university libraries, historical collections and corporate archives. Slaves haunt the pages of old letters, newspapers, receipts, payroll sheets, account books, annual reports and court records.

Ads seeking 'my Negro boy'
There are insurance policies naming their masters as beneficiaries; railroad rule books prescribing 39 lashes of the whip for recalcitrant slaves; newspapers publishing ads offering rewards for the return of "my Negro boy."

The list of corporations tied to slavery is likely to grow. Eventually, it could include energy companies that once used slaves to lay oil lines beneath Southern cities, mining companies whose slaves dug for coal and salt, tobacco marketers that relied on slaves to cultivate and cure tobacco.

Slavery's long shadow also could fall over some of Europe's oldest financial houses, which were leading financiers of the antebellum cotton trade.

Lloyd's of London, the giant insurance marketplace, could become a target because member brokerages are believed to have insured ships that brought slaves from Africa to the USA and cotton from the South to mills in New England and Britain.

The original benefactors of many of the country's top universities - Harvard, Yale, Brown, Princeton and the University of Virginia, among them - were wealthy slave owners. Lawyers on the reparations team say universities also will be sued.

Ties can be tenuous

The connection between modern-day corporations and slavery can be tenuous. Records seldom show the extent to which a given company depended on slave labor or profited from sales to slave owners. Many of the companies that are potential targets for reparation lawsuits didn't exist until after emancipation, some not until the 20th century. Instead, they bought the slave histories of other companies in corporate acquisitions over the years.

Last August, insurance giant AIG, founded 54 years after the Civil War, bought another insurer, American General. With the purchase came U.S. Life Insurance, which American General had acquired in 1997. In going through U.S. Life's archives last fall, AIG discovered that the unit had insured slaves in its early years.

Aetna first confronted allegations it had insured slaves two years ago. Since then, it has struggled to put the matter to rest, apologizing and pointing out that it funds college scholarships for African-Americans, pays for studies on racial disparities in health care and sponsors a national forum on race.

Antebellum-era slave policies "don't reflect what our company is today at all," says Aetna spokesman Fred Laberge. "We have a strong record of diversity and supporting causes and hiring."

USA TODAY contacted all the companies named in this article. Some acknowledged the evidence, others disputed it. Many declined comment. Of those that did comment, virtually all said the current company isn't liable for what happened before the Civil War.

Behind the new legal thrust is the Reparations Coordinating Committee, headed by Harvard law professor Charles Ogletree and author-activist Randall Robinson. The team includes heavyweight trial lawyers Johnnie Cochran and Dennis Sweet, and scholars such as Harvard's Cornell West, Georgetown's Richard America and Columbia's Manning Marable.

"Once the record is fleshed out and made fully available to the American people, I think companies will feel some obligation" to settle, Robinson says. "Regret's not good enough. Aetna made money, derivatively at least, from the business of slavery. . . . Aetna has to answer for that."

The legal obstacles are daunting. Slaves and their masters are dead. Company records, though sometimes damning, are seldom complete. Damages may be impossible to calculate. Most important, no company accused of profiting from slavery was breaking U.S. law at the time: Slavery was not a crime.

"We've never seen a case where someone who died hundreds of years ago can have a simple, common-law tort revived. The law wasn't designed for this," says Anthony Sebok, a tort expert at Brooklyn Law School.

Statutes of limitations on torts, or injury claims, typically last no longer than two or three years and have been extended in rare exceptions to only 30 years. Before broadening a tort case to a class-action lawsuit, reparations advocates must find the descendant of a slave damaged by one of the defendants. Then they must decide who qualifies as a slave descendant and who, in essence, is black.

The reparations team could choose instead to sue for restitution, arguing that companies were "unjustly enriched" from their use of uncompensated labor. Those cases often hinge on whether plaintiffs can give a clear, precise accounting of what was wrongfully taken from them and what they produced. That's easy when someone wants restitution for a lost object, such as a building. But how do you separate the output of slaves from that of other workers on, for example, a railroad?

Earlier reparations cases - targeting the government - have been dead ends. The group wants to avoid a repeat of Cato v. the United States, a $100 million reparations case brought against the federal government in 1995. A sympathetic U.S. Appeals Court in San Francisco dismissed the case after saying it could not find a legal basis for it. The panel said descendants of slaves must go to Congress, not the courts, to get redress for crimes against their ancestors.

That's not to say there is no precedent for reparations. Since 1995, the state of Florida has paid about $2 million in reparations to the victims of a 1923 race riot in the black settlement of Rosewood.

Ultimately, the court of public opinion could be the one that matters most. That much was clear to the German, Austrian, Swiss and French companies sued by holocaust survivors and other Europeans victimized by the Nazis.

The Holocaust cases, filed by the dozens between 1996 and 2000, were weak on the law and almost certain to be dismissed by U. S. courts. But they were corrosive to the reputations of defendant companies as long as they could linger on court dockets. The companies have settled for more than $8 billion, at the urging of the U.S. government, which mediated.

Owen Pell, a lawyer at White & Case who represented Chase Manhattan against accusations it illegally blocked accounts held by Jews in wartime France, says dozens of U.S. companies have quietly begun searching their archives in anticipation that they could be named in slavery lawsuits.

Public relations damage

The reparations movement can't win in court, Pell insists. "But companies have learned you don't judge a lawsuit by its merits. You judge it by the potential public relations damage. Corporate America is following this issue. They understand how nasty it could get if someone comes in and says you have blood on your hands."

It shouldn't come to that, says Willie Gary, a reparations team member. He says companies tied to slavery should step forward and make amends by putting money into African-American scholarships and education. "Based on what America stands for and has stood for, it's the right thing to do. There's an opportunity to make a wrong right," he says. "This should be a negotiated matter. We shouldn't be in litigation for 20 years."

Black and white Americans are sharply divided on the issue, a USA TODAY/CNN/Gallup poll shows. Big majorities of African-Americans believe companies that profited from slavery should apologize, make cash payments to descendants of slaves and set up scholarship funds for blacks. About a third of whites believe apologies and scholarships are a good idea; only 11% of whites favor cash payments to slaves' descendants.

Either way, reparation activists are preparing for a fight. Many of them battled to isolate apartheid-era South Africa and make pariahs of U.S. companies operating there in the 1980s. Expect the same bruising tactics - and some new ones - this time:

* **Pressuring shareholders.** That means demanding that pension funds and other big institutional investors dump shares of companies linked to slavery. Activists also may try forcing them to formally debate the issue at annual meetings.
* **Swaying consumers.** They will try to persuade African-Americans to pull money from accused banks and switch policies from tainted insurers.
* **Blocking mergers.** Already, they have tried to get government regulators to kill corporate deals by AIG and J.P. Morgan Chase Manhattan on the grounds the companies haven't told shareholders of potential legal liabilities stemming from any past involvement in slavery. The deals went through anyway.
* **Enlisting African-American job recruits.** The reparations group has close ties to black fraternities and sororities at the nation's colleges. It could urge graduates to shun companies accused of slave profrteering and harass corporate recruiters sent to campuses by accused companies.

The reparations team has been extraordinarily secretive. Members won't reveal the timing, corporate defendants, damages and precise legal argument of any planned lawsuits. That's partly a strategic determination to keep the opposition in the dark. Partly, it reflects unresolved disagreements among the lawyers and scholars putting the case together.

May be the last shot

With each passing day, slavery slips further into time. Gary and other trial lawyers on the team are mindful that this effort may be the last shot at addressing a historical wrong. They say their work is likely to be done pro bono. By not charging, they hope to guard against accusations they're looking to get rich by conducting corporate shakedowns.

One certainty is that new corporate cases are merely the undercard for the main event: The Holy Grail for the reparations movement is a national apology from Congress and a massive federal payout that could take the form of direct payments to African-Americans or trillions in new spending on education and social programs aimed at them. Central to any national reparations campaign is a belief that present-day gaps between whites and blacks are rooted in the past. Reparations backers argue that disparities in income, education, health, housing, divorce rates and crime grew out of the trauma of 246 years of slavery and more than a century of continuing oppression: Jim Crow laws; lynchings; job discrimination; segregation; mortgage covenants; redlining; racial profiling and other abuses.

Congress has effectively turned a deaf ear to that argument. It has stifled reparations legislation sponsored each year since 1989 by Rep. John Conyers Jr., D-Mich. But, by identifying companies that made money off slavery, reparations backers believe they can turn corporations and their CEOs into lobbyists for national restitution.

A few companies may open their checkbooks, Pell says. "What proponents of reparations are really trying to do is use the lawsuits as a tool," he says. "It's a hammer against businesses to create a call for a federal government solution."

INSURANCE FIRMS ISSUED SLAVE POLICIES

USA Today 2/21/02

Various documents link modern companies to antebellum slavery. **Reporter James Cox** takes a look at: the evidence and the companies' responses.

Early in the 19th century, insurance companies debated whether to insure slaves as property -like work animals and buildings - or as human beings. Increasingly, owners rented their slaves out to mines, railroads and tobacco processors wanted to protect their investments. Insurers eventually began issuing one-year life policies at comparatively pricey premiums that reflected the dangerous nature of the slaves' work.

USA TODAY has obtained a copy of a New York Life policy taken out on a Virginia slave by his master. The original is held by the Library of Virginia in Richmond.

In 1847, the owners of Robert Moody insured his life with Nautilus Insurance, which later changed its name to New York Life. A handwritten note on the policy says he was hired out to work at the clover Hill Pits, a coal mine near Richmond, Virginia

Evidence of 10 more New York life slave policies comes from an 1847 account book kept by the company's Natchez, Miss., agent, W.A. Britton. The book, part of a collection at Louisiana State University, contains Britton's notes on slave policies he wrote for amounts ranging from $375 to $ 600. A 1906 history of New York Life says 339 of the company's first 1,000 policies were written on the lives of slaves.

New York Life says it "thoroughly reviewed" its archives to comply with a California law requiring insurers to produce any records tying them to slavery.

It says it won't comment on what it found until the California Department of Insurance makes the records public. That's expected soon.

Deadria Farmer-Paellmann, an independent New York researcher who is documenting corporate slave connections, provided USA TODAY with a copy of an 1854 Aetna policy insuring three slaves owned by Thomas Murphy of New Orleans, LA.

The printed letterhead on the Murphy document reads "Slave Policy," and a hand notation describes it as policy No. 158, suggesting Aetna insured more than a handful of slaves.

Two years ago, Aetna expressed regret for "any involvement" it "may have" had in insuring slaves. Today, it stands by that statement and says it has been able to locate only seven policies insuring 18 slaves. "We stood up; we apologized; we tried to do the right thing;" says Aetna spokesman Fred Laberge.

Farmer-Paellmann also has connected J.P. Morgan Chase to slave insurance. Two of the many banks that merged and are part of what is today the USA's second -largest bank are listed in an 1852 circular as the banks behind a London-based consortium raising money to insure slaves.

J.P. Morgan Chase says a "thorough and extensive" search of internal and external archives turned up no evidence its predecessor banks ever did business with the consortium or that the consortium ever actually issued policies on slaves.

"We don't believe there's any basis for liability on the part of the bank," says spokeswoman Charlotte Gilbert-Biro.

In August, New York-based AIG completed the purchase of America General financial Group, a Houston-based insurer that owns U.S. Life Insurance Co. A U.S. Life policy on a Kentucky slave was preprinted in a 1935 article about slave insurance in *The American Conservationist,* a magazine.

AIG says it has "found documentation indicating" U.S.

Life insured slaves. It says slavery was a "sad and grievous chapter in American history" but won't comment further.

In the book *Black Genealogy*, historians Charles Blockson and Ron Fry wrote that before U.S. Independence, firms that were members of the Lloyd's of London market insured ships transporting slaves From Africa to the colonies.

"Of course" Lloyd's member brokers insured slaving vessels, says Declan Barriskill, a librarian responsible for the Lloyd's archives at the GuildHall Library of London. But, the records that prove it would be held by individual companies, he says.

Lloyd's, in a statements, says: "The extent of any potential involvement by Lloyd's, and indeed any financial profit or loss, are now impossible to determine. The businesses which made up Lloyd's market over 200 years ago, no longer exist and the vast majority of their records were either destroyed in a fire in 1838 or are incomplete.

Another insurer, Penn Mutual, says a search of its archives turned up two documents with information on rates for slave policies, but no evidence that the company actually insured them.

"We are very sure Penn Mutual never wrote policies on the lives of slaves" spokeswoman Pat Beauchamp says.

ACE, a Bermuda-based insurance company, says it has looked through its records as a result of suggestions that one of its divisions may have insured slave ships.

ACE says it hired a law firm, along with "leading archivist and historians, "to look into the matter.

It also compared its marine insurance records against lists of known slaving ships. The searches turned up an Aetna policy written on the life of a slave, but nothing that would implicate ACE's INA division, the company says.

"ACE believes it did not write or carry any life insurance

policy written on the life of a slave... (and) did not write or carry any policies on known slave vessels," it says.

A slave policy: New York Life, then called Nautilus Insurance, charged a Virginia slave owner a $5.81 premium plus a $1 policy fee to insure slave Robert Moody for one year in 1847. The company agreed to pay Moody's owner $412 if he was killed. Today, the premium and policy fee would be the equivalent of $145. The value of the policy, in the event of a payout, is $8,814 in today's dollars.

RAILROADS: SLAVES 'FORMED THE BACKBONE OF THE SOUTH'S RAILWAY LABOR FORCE"

USA Today 2/21/02

North America's four major rail networks - Norfolk Southern, CSX, Union Pacific and Canadian National - all own lines that were built and operated with slave labor.

Historians say nearly every rail line built east of Mississippi River and south of the Mason-Dixon line before the Civil War was constructed or run at least partly by slaves.

Ted Kornweibel, a professor of Africana Studies at San Diego State University, has documented use of slaves by 94 early rail lines. By his count: 39 now belong to Norfolk Southern, based in Norfolk, VA.; 36 are owned by CSX of Jacksonville, Fla.; 12 are part of Omaha-based Union Pacific; seven belong to Canadian National, headquartered in Montreal.

Corporate records of the time; show railroads bought slaves or leased them from their owners, usually for clearing, grading and laying tracks. Enslaved workers frequently appear in annual reports as line-item expenses, referred to variously as "hands," "colored hands," "Negro hires," "Negro property" and "slaves."

The president of Union Pacific's Memphis, El Paso & Pacific Railroad wrote to stockholders in 1858 that slaves were the "cheapest, and in the main most reliable, most easily governed' laborers.

Railroad records contain thousands of lease agreements with slave owners. A single volume of records for the Richmond Fredericksburg & Potomac Railroad now owned by CSX, covering just two months in 1850 contains 47 agreements with slave owners.

141

Slaves "formed the backbone of the South's railway labor force of track repairmen, station helpers, brakemen, firemen and sometimes even engine men," wrote University of Pennsylvania historian Walter Licht in the book *Working for the Railroad.*

Norfolk Southern declines to confirm ownership of individual rail lines from the 19th century but says it owns "80% or more" ofthe 39 identified by Kornweibel. It won't comment on whether the lines were built and run with slave labor or related questions.

CSX says it can verify the names of only a handful of the 19th century rail lines that make up its network. " As to the basic issue of reparations, we're not going to discuss that," spokeswoman Kathy Burns says.

In a statement, Canadian National said it "takes very seriously claims that slave labor" was used to build some of its early rail lines. "We are actively researching the issue. We invite any party to share with CN any relevant information or documentation."

Union Pacific says it owns nine of the 12 railroads Kornweibel identified as UP lines that owned or leased slaves. Ownership of the lines today has "no relevance" to how they were built, UP spokesman John Bromley says.

"We have no way of knowing, and we have no intention of researching that issue," Bromley says.

Slave labor: The Mobile and Girard Railroad, now owned by Norfolk Southern, advertised for slaves in 1856. Corporate records of the time show railroads bought or leased slaves.

THE RISE OF BLACK CORPORATE AMERICA

DAILY CHALLENGE
AFRO TIMES
2/19/02
By Juliet E. K. Walker

The expansion of Jim Crow laws, which enforced racial segregation, led to the establishment of Black hotels, vacation resorts, and transportation enterprises in the South as well as in the large urban ghettos in the North. Segregation and discrimination, along with Black cooperative economics, also encouraged the founding of Black financial institutions. Between 1888 and 1934, 134 Black banks were founded, including the first bank founded and headed by an America woman (Black or white), the St. Luke Penny Savings Bank, founded in Richmond, in 1903 by Maggie Lena Walker. By the early decades of the century, imposing insurance, bank, and fraternal order buildings anchored thriving urban Black business districts know as Black Wall Streets in cities such as Durham, North Carolina, and Tulsa, Oklahoma.

The establishment of Black insurance companies began to take off in early 20th century. The leading companies were the North Carolina Mutual Life Insurance Company, led by Charles C. Spaulding, and the Atlanta Life Insurance Company, founded by barber Alonzo Herndon. The early 20th century also marked the founding of Black enterprises with business receipts in the millions of dollars from products sold primarily to Black consumers. The leading Black entrepreneurs during this era were Annie Minerva Turnbo-Malone, Madame C. J. Walker, and Anthony Overton, all manufacturers of Black hair care products and cosmetics. All had sales in the millions, as did the Chicago

Defender, the Black newspaper founded by Robert Abbott.

Other Black manufacturers in the period built factories that produced dolls , apparel, furniture, mortuary supplies and caskets, electrical appliances, and chemicals. There was even a Black automobile manufacturer. Black business people such as filmmaker Ocar Micheaux and Harry Pace of Black Swan Records tried to capitalize on the new motion picture and recording industries. Given the diversity and success of these varied enterprises, the first three decades of 20th century are considered the golden age of Black business. The period marked the first wave in the rise of Back leaders at the time described as a "separate Black economy," a result of white racism in a free-enterprise economy.

The leading Black economic nationalists of the era, including the rivals W. E. B. Du Bois and Booker T. Washington, encouraged Black consumer support of Black business. While Du Bois focused on the scholarly study of Black economic activity with his 1899 Atlanta conference on "The Negro in Business," Washington in 1900 founded the National Negro Business League. Other Black business organizations followed. Black bankers, Black insurance executives, Black funeral directors, and Black merchants all established groups to promote the professionalization and advancement of their business activities. In the 1920s, the Universal Negro Improvement Association (UNIA) of Marcus Garvey established various Black nationalist business enterprises, including the Negro Factories Corporation and the Black Star Line, a steamship company.

Editor's note: *Many, many billions of dollars have been lost by the African American communities in the United States over the years from post slavery to present day, from inventions, science and industry.*

Revelations - Rod Ivey

BLACK AMERICANS IN INVENTION

Were it not for Black American inventors, we would not be wearing long lasting, comfortable, inexpensive shoes, or enjoying perishable food shipped from distant places nor would our firemen have gas masks to prevent them from inhaling smoke.

Black astronomer, mathematician Benjamin Banneker constructed the first clock in America in 1761. The first Black to receive a patent was Henry Blair who invented the corn harvester in 1834. In 1857, Andrew J. Beard received $50,000 for an invention ..."Jenny Coupler" an automatic device securing cars by merely bumping them together..'. preventing countless deaths of railroadmen.

Lynn, Massachusetts became the shoe capital of the world as a result of Jan Matzeliger's shoe lasting machine patented in 1883. The expression "the real McCoy" was used to describe one machine patented by Elijah McCoy, who developed some 51 devices for lubricating heavy machinery. The forerunner of the modern incubator, which can hatch 50,000 eggs at a time, was patented by Granville Wood, in 1887.

The first textbooks on the lighting system used by the Edison Electric Co. of N.Y. were written by Lewis Latimer who also patented the first incandescent light bulb with a carbon filament in 1881.

Inventor Garrett A. Morgan had to masquerade as an Indian to get recognition even though his gas masks saved the lives of men trapped in a tunnel explosion 203 feet below Lake Erie. In 1923, he received $40,000 from the General Electric Corp. for his automatic traffic signal. Frederick McKinley Jones,is credited with ...the first refrigeration system for long haul trucks...a portable X-ray machine and an air conditioning unit for military hospitals.

Reprinted from the Journal of The Patent Office Society, Vol. 62, No.2, February 1980

BLACK INVENTIONS

CRAFTSMAN® Sprinklers

Lawn Sprinkler
By Joseph H.Smith
May 4th 1897
Patent 581,785

Electric Lights --
Lewis Latimer 1882

ountain Pen
.B.Purvis
an.7,1890
atent NR.419,065

AUTOMATIC TRANSMISSION
R.B.Spikes
1933-Dec.17th.
Patent N.R. 1,936,996

THE FOLDING CHAIR
A.B.Blackburn
July 1899

First Clock in America --
Benjamin Banneker
1761

Shoe Making Machine -- Jan Matzeliger
March 20, 1883

Telephone -- Granville Woods
1880

ary Machine -- A.J. Bread
July 16, 1899

Battery--Granville Woods

WATER-PROOFER PAINT & Varnish
Percy L. Julian

M. E. BENJAMIN.
GONG AND SIGNAL CHAIR FOR HOTELS, &c.

No. 386,289.   Patented July 17, 1888.

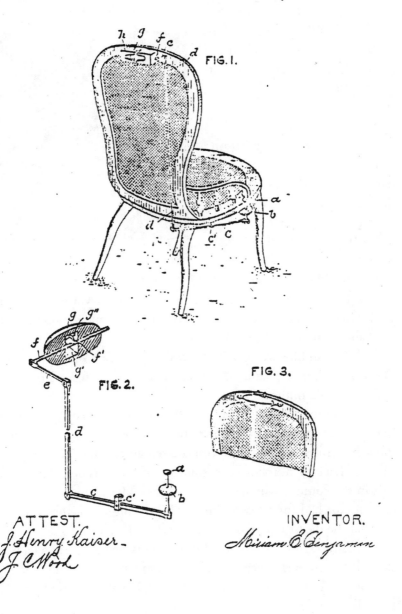

FIG. 1.

FIG. 2.

FIG. 3.

ATTEST.
J. Henry Kaiser.
J. C. Wood.

INVENTOR.
Miriam E. Benjamin

SOMETIMES IT DOES TAKE A ROCKET SCIENTIST

ASSOCIATED PRESS
Saturday, February 13, 1999; Page V02

SMYRNA, Ga.—This is a reading comprehension exercise for children. It is written by Susan Fineman, a reading specialist in the New Haven, Conn., school district.

Lonnie Johnson

On Lonnie Johnson's office wall, right next to his patents for a thermostat, hair-drying rollers and a wet diaper detector, is patent No. 4,757,946 - for the flow actuated pulsator.

The Super Soaker, as it's known to millions, is a little more advanced than your typical water gun. This high-powered weapon has drenched many backyard warriors and revitalized the toy gun market.

And unlike his work in the design of three NASA space probes that earned him a plaque, this homemade gadget turned the rocket scientist into a millionaire.

Johnson's career began in 1968 when the native of Mobile, Ala., won a state science fair competition with Liner, a remote-control robot he built using batteries, compressed air and tape reels.

"Back then, robots were unheard of, so I was one of only a few kids in the country who had his own robot," he said.

Not bad for a black child who growing up in the South was told that he didn't have what it took to be an engineer.

Although disheartened, Johnson persevered, receiving a bachelor's degree in mechanical engineering and a master's in nuclear engineering. He holds wide-ranging patents - 49 in all - and is working on an additional dozen or so.

As an engineer at the National Aeronautics and Space Administration's acclaimed Jet Propulsion Laboratory in Pasadena, Calif., Johnson worked on Voyager, Mars Observer and Galileo.

At the time of his most lucrative stroke of creative genius, in 1982, Johnson was an engineer at the Strategic Air Command in Omaha, Neb., working in his spare time on a new type of heat pump that would use water instead of Freon.

He hooked up a model of the pump to the bathroom sink in his home.

"I turned around, and I was shooting this thing across the bathroom into the tub, and the stream of water was so powerful that the curtains were swirling in the breeze it sent out," he said. "I thought,'This would make a great water gun.' "

The Super Soaker, for which Johnson received a patent in 1988, was introduced into the market in 1990 with a pumped-up reservoir capable of firing a stream of water up to 50 feet. It blew away plain old water pistols.

Today, more than 250 million of the high-tech water weapons have been sold, according to Al Davis, Larami executive vice president.

"That's four guns to every kid in the United States," Davis said, noting that the plastic toys also found a surprise market among adults.

Bibliography

Anekwe Simon, "His Invention Keeps Drivers From Sleeping" <u>Amsterdam News</u>, February 7, 1984 (newspaper article)

"Black Innovators" <u>Journal Of The Patent Office Society</u>, Volume 62, No. 2, February, 1980.

"Black Americans in Invention" <u>Journal of The Patent Office Society</u>, Volume 62, No. 2, February, 1990

Brown, J. Zamgbwa, "Jersey Genius Invents Solar Hot Water System That Works", <u>Amsterdam News</u>, August 27, 1994

Coleman, Chrisena, "She Gives Science Boost", <u>New York Daily News</u>, April 25, 1996, (newspaper article on Dr. Mae Jemison).

Connors, Cathy "Black Physicist Dies: Prized Discoveries Propelled U.S. Into Space Race", <u>Amsterdam News</u>, April 4, 1994 (newspaper article)

Cox, James "Activist Challenge Corporations That They Say Are Tied To Slavery", <u>USA Today</u>, February 21, 2002.

"Insurance Firms Issued Slave Policies", (article by James Cox, author of the previous entry) February 21, 2002

"Railroads: Slaves Formed The Backbone Of The South's Railway Labor Force", (article by James Cox, author of the previous entry)

Crawford, Marc, "Washington Sends For Detroit", <u>Jet Magazine</u> P.84 (magazine article)

DeRamus, Betty, "It's The Ones We Don't Hear About Who Are The Greats" <u>Detroit News</u> (newspaper article)

"Exceptional Black Scientists" (Publication Of The CIBA-GEIGY Corp.) 1985 (pamphlet)

The Howard University Africana Series

Garvey, Amy J. "Philosophy and Opinions Of The Honorable Marcus Garvey", Vol. 2, 1925

"Johnson Named Dean Of Howard University School Of Engineering" Amsterdam News, July 6, 1996.

Muhammad, Richard, "Dr. Justice Leads Fight Against AIDS in Black Community", The Final Call, June 15, 1992 (newspaper article)

Pruitt, William, "Kenyan Scientist Makes Historical AIDS Treatment Breakthrough" (The American Black Male) September 1990

"Some Claims That Have Been Made About The Use Of Kemron" {article by William Pruitt, author of the previous entry)

"Sometimes It Takes A Rocket Scientist", Associated Press, February 13, 1999

"Support Grows for Mathematician Gabriel Oyibo", Our Time Press, August 2000, (newspaper article)

Templeton, William ," Black Manufacturers Continue to Make An Impact", Daily Challenge, April 7, 1998 (newspaper article)

"Two Sisters Ages 10 and 8 Invent Bug Killing Spray" Amsterdam News, July 29, 1989 (newspaper article)

Walker, Juliet E.K., The Rise Of Black Corporate America", Daily Challenge, February 19, 2002 (newspaper article)

Appendix A

LIST OF BLACK INVENTORS AND INVENTIONS

Inventor	Invention	Date	Paten
Abrams, W.B.	Hame Attachment	Apr. 14, 1891	450,5
Allen, C.W.	Self-Leveling Table	Nov. 1, 1895	613,4
Allen, J.B.	Clothes Line Support	Dec. 10, 1895	551,1
Ashbourne, A.P.	Process for Preparing Cocoanut for Domestic Use	June 1, 1875	163,9
Ashbourne, A.P.	Biscuit Cutter	Nov. 30, 1875	170,4
Ashbourne, A.P.	Refining Cocoanut Oil	July 27, 1880	230,5
Ashbourne, A.P.	Process of Treating Cocoanut	Aug. 21, 1877	194,2
Bailes, Wm.	Ladder Scaffold Support	Aug. 5, 1879	218,1
Bailey, L.C.	Combined Truss and Bandage	Sept. 25, 1883	285,5
Bailey, L.C.	Folding Bed	July 18, 1899	629,2
Bailiff, C.O.	Shampoo Headrest	Oct. 11, 1898	612,0
Ballow, W.J.	Combined Hatrack and Table	Mar. 19, 1898	601,4
Barnes, G.A.E.	Design for Sign	Aug. 19, 1898	29,1
Beard, A.J.	Car Coupler	Nov. 23, 1897	594,0
Beard, A.J.	Rotary Engine	July 5, 1892	478,2
Becket, G.E.	Letter Box	Oct. 4, 1892	483,5
Bell, L.	Locomotive Smoke Stack	May 23, 1871	115,1
Bell, L.	Dough Kneader	Dec. 10, 1872	133,8
Benjamin, L.W.	Broom Moisteners and Bridles	May 16, 1893	497,7
Benjamin, M.E.	Gong and Signal Chairs for Hotels	July 17, 1888	386,2
Binga, M.W.	Street Sprinkling Apparatus	July 22, 1879	217,8
Blackburn, A.B.	Railway Signal	Jan. 10, 1888	376,3
Blackburn, A.B.	Spring Seat for Chairs	Apr. 3, 1888	380,4
Blackburn, A.B.	Cash Carrier	Oct. 23, 1888	391,5
Blair, Henry	Corn Planter	Oct. 14, 1834	
Blair, Henry	Cotton Planter	Aug. 31, 1836	
Blue, L.	Hand Corn Shelling Device	May 20, 1884	298,9
Booker, L.F.	Design for Rubber Scraping Knife	Mar. 28, 1899	30,4
Boone, Sarah	Ironing Board	Apr. 26, 1892	473,6
Bowman, H.A.	Method for Making Flags	Feb. 23, 1892	469,3
Brooks, C.B.	Punch	Oct. 31, 1893	507,6
Brooks, C.B.	Street Sweepers	Mar. 17, 1896	556,7
Brooks, C.B.	Street Sweepers	May 12, 1896	560,15
Brooks, Hallstead and Page	Street Sweepers	April 21, 1896	558,7
Brown, Henry	Receptacle for Storing and Preserving Papers	Nov. 2, 1886	352,0
Brown, L.F.	Bridle Bit	Oct. 25, 1892	484,99
Brown, O.E.	Horeshoe	Aug. 23, 1892	481,27
Brown & Latimer	Water Closets for Railway Cars	Feb. 10, 1874	147,36
Burr, J.A.	Lawn Mower	May 9, 1899	624,74
Burr, W.F.	Switching Device for Railways	Oct. 31, 1899	636,19
Burwell, W.	Boot or Shoe	Nov. 28, 1899	638,14
Butler, R.A.	Train Alarm	June 15, 1897	584,54
Butts, J.W.	Luggage Carrier	Oct. 10, 1899	634,61
Byrd, T.J.	Improvement in Holders for Reins for Horses	Feb. 6, 1872	123,32
Byrd, T.J.	Apparatus for Detaching Horses from Carriages	Mar. 19, 1872	124,79
Byrd, T.J.	Improvement in Neck Yokes for Wagons	Apr. 30, 1872	126,18
Byrd, T.J.	Improvement in Car Couplings	Dec. 1, 1874	157,37

153

LIST OF BLACK INVENTORS AND INVENTIONS

Inventor	Invention	Date	Pa#
Haines, J.H.	Portable Basin	Sept. 28, 1897	590
Hammonds, J.F.	Apparatus for Holding Yarn Skeins	Dec. 15, 1896	572
Harding, F.H.	Extension Banquet Table	Nov. 22, 1898	614
Hawkins, J.	Gridiron	Mar. 26, 1845	3
Hawkins, R.	Harness Attachment	Oct. 4, 1887	370
Headen, M.	Foot Power Hammer	Oct. 5, 1886	350
Hearness, R.	Sealing Attachment for Bottles	Feb. 15, 1898	598
Hearness, R.	Detachable Car Fender	July 4, 1899	628
Hilyer, A.F.	Water Evaporator Attachment for Hot Air Registers	Aug. 26, 1890	435
Hilyer, A.F.	Registers	Oct. 14, 1890	438
Holmes, E.H.	Gage	Nov. 12, 1895	549
Hunter, J.H.	Portable Weighing Scales	Nov. 3, 1896	570
Hyde, R.N.	Composition for Cleaning and Preserving Carpets	Nov. 6, 1888	392
Jackson, B.F.	Heating Apparatus	Mar. 1, 1898	599
Jackson, B.F.	Matrix Drying Apparatus	May 10, 1898	603
Jackson, B.F.	Gas Burner	Apr. 4, 1899	622
Jackson, H.A.	Kitchen Table	Oct. 6, 1896	569
Jackson, W.H.	Railway Switch	Mar. 9, 1897	578
Jackson, W.H.	Railway Switch	Mar. 16, 1897	593
Jackson, W.H.	Automatic Locking Switch	Aug. 23, 1898	609
Johnson, I.R.	Bicycle Frame	Oct. 10, 1899	634
Johnson, P.	Swinging Chairs	Nov. 15, 1881	249
Johnson, P.	Eye Protector	Nov. 2, 1880	234
Johnson, W.	Velocipede	June 20, 1899	627
Johnson, W.A.	Paint Vehicle	Dec. 4, 1888	393
Johnson, W.H.	Overcoming Dead Centers	Feb. 4, 1896	554
Johnson, W.H.	Overcoming Dead Centers	Oct. 11, 1898	612
Johnson, W.	Egg Beater	Feb. 5, 1884	292
Jones, F.M.	Ticket Dispensing Machine	June 27, 1939	2,163
Jones, F.M.	Air Conditioning Unit	July 12, 1949	2,475
Jones, F.M.	Method for Air Conditioning	Dec. 7, 1954	2,696
Jones, F.M.	Method for Preserving Perishables	Feb. 12,1957	2,789
Jones, F.M.	Two-Cycle Gasoline Engine	Nov. 28, 1950	2,523
Jones, F.M.	Two-Cycle Gas Engine	May 29, 1945	2,376
Jones, F.M.	Starter Generator	July 12, 1949	2,475
Jones, F.M.	Starter Generator for Cooling Gas Engines	July 12, 1949	2,475
Jones, F.M.	Two-Cycle Gas Engine	Mar. 11, 1947	2,417
Jones, F.M.	Means for Thermostatically Operating Gas Engines	July 26, 1949	2,477
Jones, F.M.	Rotary Compressor	Apr. 18, 1950	2,504
Jones, F.M.	System for Controlling Operation of Refrigeration Units	May 23, 1950	2,509
Jones, F.M.	Apparatus for Heating or Cooling Atmosphere within an Enclosure	Oct. 24, 1950	2,526
Jones, F.M.	Prefabricated Refrigerator Construction	Dec. 26, 1950	2,535
Jones, F.M.	Refrigeration Control Device	Jan. 8, 1952	2,581
Jones, F.M.	Methods and Means of Defrosting a Cold Diffuser	Jan. 19, 1954	2,666
Jones, F.M.	Control Device for Internal Combustion Enginer	Sept. 2,1958	2,850
Jones, F.M.	Thermostat and Temperature Control System	Feb. 23, 1960	2,926
Jones, F.M.	Removable Cooling Units for Compartments		2,336
Jones, F.M.	Means for Automatically Stopping and Starting Gas Engines ("J.A. Numero et al")	Dec. 21, 1943	2,337
Jones, F.M.	Design for Air Conditioning Unit	July 4, 1950	159
Jones, F.M.	Design for Air Conditioning Unit	Apr. 28, 1942	132
Jones & Long	Caps for Bottles	Sept. 13, 1898	610
Joyce, J.A.	Ore Bucket	Apr. 26, 1898	603

LIST OF BLACK INVENTORS AND INVENTIONS

entor	Invention	Date	Patent
imer & Brown	Water Closets for Railway Cars	Feb. 10, 1874	147,363
imer, L.H.	Manufacturing Carbons	June 17, 1882	252,386
imer, L.H.	Apparatus for Cooling and Disinfecting	Jan. 12, 1886	334,078
imer, L.H.	Locking Racks for Coats, Hats and Umbrellas	Mar. 24, 1896	557,076
imer & Nichols	Electric Lamp	Sept. 13, 1881	247,097
imer & Tregoning	Globe Support for Electric Lamps	Mar. 21, 1882	255,212
valette, W.A.	Printing Press	Sept. 17,, 1878	208,208
, H.	Animal Trap	Feb. 12,, 1867	61,,941
, J.	Kneading Machine	Aug. 7, 1894	524,042
,, J.	Break Crumbing Machine	June 4, 1895	540,553
lie, F.W.	Envelope Seal	Sept. 21, 1897	590,325
rray, W.	Attachment for Bicycles	Jan. 27, 1891	445,452
nce, L.	Game Apparatus	Dec. 1, 1891	464,935
sh, H.H.	Life Preserving Stool	Oct. 5, 1875	168,519
wman, L.D.	Brush	Nov. 15, 1898	614,
wson, S.	Oil Heater or Cooker	May 22, 1894	520,188
chols & Latimer	Electric Lamp	Sept. 13, 1881	247,097
ckerson, W.J.	Mandolin and Guitar Attachment for Pianos	June 27, 1899	627,739
Connor & Turner	Alarm for Boilers	Aug. 25, 1896	566,612
Connor & Turner	Steam Gage	Aug. 25, 1896	566,613
Connor & Turner	Alarm for Containing Vessels	Feb. 8, 1898	598,572
tlaw, J.W.	Horseshoes	Nov. 15, 1898	614,273
rryman, F.R.	Caterers' Tray Table	Feb. 2, 1892	468,038
terson, H.	Attachment for Lawn Mowers	Apr. 30, 1889	402,189
elps, W.H.	Apparatus for Washing Vehicles	Mar. 23, 1897	579,242
ckering, J.F.	Air Ship	Feb. 20, 1900	643,975
ckett, H.	Scaffold	June 30, 1874	152,511
nn, T.B.	File Holder	Aug. 17, 1880	231,355
lk, A.J.	Bicycle Support	Apr. 14, 1896	558,103
igsley, A.	Blind Stop	July 29, 1890	433,306
irdy & Peters	Design for Spoons	Apr. 23, 1895	24,228
irdy & Sadgwar	Folding Chair	June 11, 1889	405,117
irdy, W.	Device for Sharpening Edged Tools	Oct. 27, 1896	570,337
irdy, W.	Design for Sharpening Edged Tools	Aug. 16, 1898	609,267
irdy, W.	Device for Sharpening Edged Tools	Aug. 1, 1899	630,106
irvis, W.B.*	Bag Fastener	Apr. 25, 1882	256,856
irvis, W.B.	Hand Stamp	Feb. 27, 1883	273,149
irvis, W.B.	Fountain Pen	Jan. 7, 1890	419,065
irvis, W.B.	Magnetic Car Balancing Device	May 21, 1895	539,542
irvis, W.B.	Electric Railway Switch	Aug. 17, 1897	588176

Purvis also patented ten paper bag machines between 1884 and 1894.)

| Queen, W. | Guard for Companion Ways and Hatches | Aug. 18, 1891 | 458,131 |

(Some patents are not included here because of current litigation; or because they were so basic in nature that redesigning and refiling procedures are now in process.)

Inventor	Invention		Date	Pa#
Ray, E.P.	Chair Support Device		Feb. 21, 1899	62
Ray, L.P.	Dust Pan		Aug. 3, 1897	58
Reed, J.W.	Dough Kneader and Roller		Sept. 23, 1884	30
Reynolds, H.H.	Window Ventilator for Railroad Cars		Apr. 3, 1883	27
Reynolds, H.H.	Safety Gate for Bridges		Oct. 7, 1890	43
Reynolds, R.R.	Non-Refillable Bottle		May 2, 1899	62
Rhodes, J.B.	Water Closets		Dec. 19, 1899	63
Richardson, A.C.	Hame Fastener		Mar. 14, 1882	25
Richardson, A.C.	Churn		Feb. 17, 1891	44
Richardson, A.C.	Casket Lowering Device		Nov. 13, 1894	52
Richardson, A.C.	Insect Destroyer		Feb. 28, 1899	62
Richardson, A.C.	Bottle		Dec. 12, 1899	63
Richardson, W.H.	Cotton Chopper		June 1, 1886	34
Richardson, W.H.	Child's Carriage		June 18, 1889	40
Richardson, W.H.	Child's Carriage		June 18, 1889	40
Richey, C.V.	Car Coupling		June 15, 1897	584
Richey, C.V.	Railroad Switch		Aug. 3, 1897	587
Richey, C.V.	Railroad Switch		Oct. 26, 1897	592
Richey, C.V.	Fire Escape Bracket		Dec. 28, 1897	592
Richey, C.V.	Combined Hammock and Stretcher		Dec. 13, 1898	615
Rickman, A.L.	Overshoe		Feb. 8, 1898	598
Ricks, J.	Horseshoe		Mar. 30, 1886	338
Ricks, J.	Overshoes for Horses		June 6, 1899	626
Rillieux, N.	Sugar Refiner (Evaporating Pan)		Dec. 10, 1846	4
Robinson, E.R.	Casting Composite		Nov. 23, 1897	594
Robinson, E.R.	Electric Railway Trolley		Sept. 19, 1893	505
Robinson, J.H.	Life Saving Guards for Locomotives		Mar. 14, 1899	621
Robinson, J.H.	Life Saving Guards for Street Cars		Apr. 25, 1899	623
Robinson, J.	Dinner Pail		Feb. 1, 1887	356,
Romain, A.	Passenger Register		Apr. 23, 1889	402
Ross, A.L.	Runner for Stops		Aug. 4, 1896	565,
Ross, A.L.	Bag Closure		June 7, 1898	605,
Ross, A.L.	Trousers Support		Nov. 28, 1899	638,
Ross, J.	Bailing Press		Sept. 5, 1899	632,
Roster, D.N.	Feather Curler		Mar. 10, 1896	556,
Ruffin, S.	Vessels for Liquids and Manner of Sealing		Nov. 20, 1899	737,
Russell, L.A.	Guard Attachment for Beds		Aug. 13, 1895	544,
Sampson, G.T.	Sled Propeller		Feb. 17, 1885	312,
Sampson, G.T.	Clothes Drier		June 7, 1892	476,
Scottron, S.R.	Adjustable Window Cornice		Feb. 17, 1880	224,
Scottron, S.R.	Cornice		Jan. 16, 1883	270,
Scottron, S.R.	Pole Tip		Sept. 31, 1886	349,
Scottron, S.R.	Curtain Rod		Aug. 30, 1892	481,
Scottron, S.R.	Sleeping Car Berth Register		Sept. 12, 1893	505,
Shanks, S.C.	Supporting Bracket		July 21, 1897	587,
Shewcraft, F.	Letter Box	Detroit, Michigan		
Shorter, D.W.	Feed Rack		May 17, 1887	363,
Smith, J.W.	Improvement in Games		Apr. 17, 1900	647,
Smith, J.W.	Lawn Sprinkler		May 4, 1897	581,
Smith, J.W.	Lawn Sprinkler		Mar. 22, 1898	601,
Smith, P.D.	Potato Digger		Jan. 21, 1891	445,
Smith, P.D.	Grain Binder		Feb. 23, 1892	469,
Snow & Johns	Linament		Oct. 7, 1890	437,
Spears, H.	Portable Shield for Infantry		Dec. 27, 1870	110,
Spikes, R.B.	Combination Milk Bottle Opener and Bottle Cover		June 29, 1926	1,590,5
Spikes, R.B.	Method and Apparatus for Obtaining Average Samples and Temperature of Tank Liquids		Oct. 27, 1931	1,828,7
Spikes, R.B.	Automatic Gear Shift		Dec. 6, 1932	1,889,8
Spikes, R.B.	Transmission and Shifting Thereof		Nov. 28, 1933	1,936,9
Spikes, R.B.	Self-Locking Rack for Billiard Cues		Around 1910	Not Foun
Spikes, R.B.	Automatic Shoe Shine Chair		Around 1939	Not Foun
Spikes, R.B.	Multiple Barrel Machine Gun		Around 1940	Not Foun

Appendix B

Name	Invention
Alexander, Louis	Burglar Alarm
Alexander, Louis	TV Tubs
Allen, Harrison	Ignition of Solid Propellent Rocket
Banks, Charles	Spark Plug
Benton, J. W.	Derrick for Hoisting
Boker David	Inner Tube
Bowman, Henry	Flags
Boykin, Otis	Control Unit for Artificial Heart Stimulator
Boykin, Otis	Electrical Device Used on All Guided Missiles and IBM Computers
Brown, Solomon	Assisted Morse in Development of Telegraph Devise
Bryant, Charles	Auto Seat Bed
Carruthers, George	Ultraviolet Spectograph
Cassel, Oscar	Flight Machine (1923)
Douglas, William	Various Invention for Harvesting
Dyer, Wilbert	Satellite Tracker
Gourdine , Meredith	Device to Directly Convert Gas into High Voltage Electricity
Gourdine , Meredith	Exhaust purification Device for Automobiles
Gourdine , Meredith	Air Pollution Measuring Device
Gourdine , Meredith	Generators for Power Stations.
Hale	Automobile (1928)

Name	Invention
Hall, Lloyd	Asphalt
Harper, Solomon	Blocking System for Controlling Railway Trains
Helm, Tony	All Angle Wrench Attachment
Johnson	Compound Engine
Johnson	Water Boiler
Johnson	Bread Kneading Machine
Johnson, Paul	Therapeutic Lamps
Larry, Clarence	Camera (takes pictures of moving eye)
Lavalette	Two Printing Presses